D1126393

Behaviour Modification in the Classroom

Alex Harrop

HODDER AND STOUGHTON
LONDON SYDNEY AUCKLAND TORONTO

British Library Cataloguing in Publication Data

Harrop, Alex
Behaviour modification in the classroom.
1. Educational psychology
2. Behaviour modification
I. Title
371.1'024 LB1051

ISBN 0 340 28172 3

First published 1983

Printed and bound in Great Britain for
Hodder and Stoughton Educational,
a division of Hodder and Stoughton Ltd,
Mill Road, Dunton Green, Sevenoaks, Kent,
by Biddles Ltd, Guildford, Surrey.
Photoset by Rowland Phototypesetting Ltd,
Bury St Edmunds, Suffolk.

Contents

Introduction

This book is intended to be of practical help to serving teachers and teachers-in-training. The overall purpose is to inform the reader of the applications of behaviour modification in ordinary schools. As the title of the opening chapter ('Some Typical Pupils') may suggest, the book is concerned with actual, observed pupil behaviour rather than with mere speculation or theorizing about the hypothetical causes of such behaviour.

I have resisted the temptation to trace the academic 'pre-history' of behaviour modification, since, in my view, the really significant and systematic application of its principles and procedures in the classrooms of ordinary schools is primarily a feature of the last two decades.

This period has seen the development of, and some refinement upon, such early investigations as that of Madsen, Becker and Thomas (1968), in which the selective use of teacher attention, combined with a clear statement of classroom rules, was shown to reduce the disruptive behaviour of certain pupils in two classrooms.

This book also pays close attention to ways in which teachers can manage 'difficult' pupils. Here, however, pupils are regarded as having 'difficulties' rather than as merely being 'difficult'. In other words, the emphasis is upon removing difficulties, rather than upon 'containing' difficult pupils.

The text is not, however, restricted to a consideration of the means by which pupils who experience difficulties may be helped. It goes beyond this, and suggests ways in which teachers can promote the optimum development of all the pupils in their classrooms. The book includes a variety of examples, and it is hoped that these will both illustrate the flexibility of behaviour modification techniques and provoke discussions between teachers and intending teachers.

And since teaching a class is a dynamic process involving pupils and teacher alike, the modification of pupils' behaviour must involve a modification of teacher behaviour. For that reason, this book may – from a certain angle – be viewed as a text in educational psychology which is concerned with the teacher as much as with the pupil. More immediately, however, it has four basic aims:

1 To acquaint the reader with the kinds of pupil behaviour to which behaviour modification techniques have been applied.

2 To outline and discuss the fundamental principles and practices of behaviour modification, and their relation to current and customary school procedures.
3 To describe and analyse some of the ways in which behaviour modification has been used in schools, especially those schools within the British education system.
4 To suggest and consider some ways in which teachers can use their own professional skills within the framework of behaviour modification, and in the context of the educational system, to alleviate difficulties experienced by their pupils.

NOTE: Readers should understand that, throughout this text, in paragraphs referring to the teacher or pupil in general terms, for simplicity of style 'he' should be taken to subsume 'she'.

Acknowledgments

In writing this book I have been influenced by many people in a variety of ways. Above all, I owe a debt of gratitude to those teachers who have attended in-services courses in behaviour modification, and have put the procedures to the test. This debt, however, extends beyond the teachers' involvement as practitioners; they have also taught me a great deal by their skilled interpretations and evaluations. In this respect, the influence of Joe Ling, Barbara Moore and Barry Mees has been of particular value.

At one step removed from the work-face, I owe much to Nancy Crawford, Colin Critchley and Eddie McNamara for their inspiration, and beyond this personal level, I am indebted to numerous behaviour modification investigators, particularly those whose work is summarized in the text. In preparing this book, I have had considerable help from Geoff Farrell, Bill Costigan and Frank McNeill, each of whom has made many valuable suggestions.

Finally, my thanks to my wife Sally, and my sons Bill, Mike and Mark, without whose tolerance and good-humoured acceptance of my periodic withdrawal from family life, this book would not have been completed.

Chapter 1

Some Typical Pupils

This chapter consists essentially of a collection of cases. Each case is the story of the treatment of a pupil whose behaviour was a source of concern to his or her teacher. The cases have been selected for their diversity, but they do have certain features in common. In each one, the pupil was treated in his own classroom by the teacher. Advice was sought, discussions took place, but finally it was the teacher who decided on the treatment to be used.

The cases are of necessity summarized. This does tend to remove from them all traces of the lengthy deliberations and sensitive judgements which were involved. Yet it must be said that without the teachers' understanding of their pupils, and of the dynamics of their particular situations, the outcomes of these cases would have been very different.

There is a danger when these cases are read that the teachers may be seen to be applying prescriptions to their pupils, and that the treatment may be seen to be mechanical and lacking in humanity. The reality is very different. It is true that teachers have had to be consistent in their treatment, but it is equally true that none of these pupils would have been treated if their teachers had not been concerned about their progress.

The cases presented here have been chosen to cover a broad spectrum. Six come from the writer's direct experience with teachers, and two were added after discussions with a colleague. Each case is the result of many interlinked factors. Although it is not a very informative statement to make, each case depended upon variables within the pupil, within the teacher, and within the classroom context. Which of these surfaced in any one case depended primarily upon the teacher's professional judgement of a particular set of circumstances. It is not really possible to be more specific than this.

A relatively bare outline of each case is given. The main aims in presenting each case are as follows:

1 to sketch in the kinds of behaviour which caused the teacher some concern;
2 to show how the teacher obtained an estimate of the incidence of this behaviour, by obtaining what is technically known as a baseline measure;

3 to show how the teacher treated the behaviour; and
4 to indicate what were the results of the treatment.

In each case, the names of the pupil and the teacher have been altered to preserve anonymity.

Each case is followed by a comment or two, so that some of the more important features may be emphasized. Technical terms have been kept to a minimum to ensure smooth communication, except when it was felt that the introduction of a term made for easier reading.

It should become apparent when reading these cases that behaviour modification is very much a practical approach to teaching which is concerned with treating the behaviour of pupils, rather than speculating about untreatable causes. It does not allow the teacher to opt out of responsibility. One cannot simply attribute a pupil's problems to his home environment or to physiological abnormalities, and wash one's hands of his behaviour. This is not to say that such considerations are irrelevant. They are very relevant, and are taken into consideration when a teacher considers treatment. Teachers usually have a good knowledge of home environments, and if physiological abnormalities are suspected, these can be investigated by going through the appropriate procedures.

It may well be, however, that there are pupils in some classes who seem unresponsive to any treatment their teachers are able to offer. Under these circumstances, it is prudent to consider whether these pupils really belong in the classes, and to consult with the relevant agencies, particularly the Schools' Psychological Service. If the pupils do not belong in the classes, then treatment is best applied in the classes in which they do belong. If the pupils do belong in the classes, then this is where they ought to be treated. The cases included in this chapter illustrate some of the various ways in which a teacher can successfully treat a pupil in his own classroom.

The cases are presented in no discernible order. They vary across too many dimensions for this to be possible. The pupils' ages range from six to fourteen, and the behaviours treated vary from 'bullying' to 'work output'. Some of the pupils have fairly common behaviour problems; other problems are very rare.

The comments made are sequential, so that the reader will gain maximum benefit by reading the cases in the order in which they are presented.

Frank

Frank was a primary school pupil aged eight. His teacher Mrs Jones, said he was above average in intelligence for his class, but he did little work. Frank was mischievous and full of fun. He frequently interrupted other pupils when they were working, either by talking to them, or by 'pulling funny faces' at them. He had a knack of losing pencils and books, and had the rather unusual habit of continually checking with the teacher and with the other pupils, to find out what he was supposed to be doing.

When Mrs Jones was talking with the class, Frank behaved well. It was only when work was set for the class that he began to cause difficulties. Mrs Jones was concerned about Frank's behaviour not because she minded him being a nuisance, but because he was not learning as well as he could. She was also worried because his behaviour was distracting the other pupils.

The first step before treating Frank was to obtain an accurate estimate of the incidence of these inappropriate behaviours. On ten successive school days, Mrs Jones set aside ten minutes when she would normally mark books, when the pupils were working, and kept an eye on Frank's behaviour. She continued to mark her books, but unobtrusively noted each time Frank's behaviour could be classified into one of the following categories:

1 verbal interruption of other pupils when they were working;
2 pulling faces at other pupils;
3 losing pencil or book;
4 checking with teacher or other pupil.

By the end of these ten days, a good estimate of Frank's inappropriate behaviour had been gained, and treatment began.

Immediately after obtaining this estimate, Mrs Jones took a lesson with the class in which she discussed the rules of the classroom. Amongst the rules, the undesirability of verbal interruption, pulling faces, losing pencils and books, and checking up on work set, was pointed out, although no specific reference was made to Frank.

Following this lesson, Mrs Jones began to pay attention to Frank as often as possible when he was doing his work, and to ignore him as much as possible when he behaved inappropriately. She continued to measure his behaviour for the same ten minutes each day. This method of treating Frank continued for four weeks.

By the end of these four weeks, Mrs Jones noted that Frank's behaviour had improved considerably, and that he had begun to show much more interest in his work. The data she had obtained by observing Frank supported this view. Frank had been averaging between five and six instances of inappropriate behaviour every ten minutes before treatment, and was averaging between one and two such instances by the end of the fourth week.

COMMENT Pupils like Frank are by no means unusual in the classroom. Compared with many pupils in other classes, they are not even regarded as causing problems. However, for Mrs Jones, who had been teaching for twenty-five years, Frank's behaviour was a real problem. The learning in her classroom was being diminished by Frank's behaviour.

There are three main elements in the method used by Mrs Jones to treat Frank. These are 'rules, attention and ignoring'. Mrs Jones spent a lesson making the rules clear to the class, and during this lesson she pointed out how Frank's behaviour infringed these rules, although she did not directly refer to him. Following this, she paid attention whenever she could to Frank when he was working and ignored him whenever he behaved inappropriately. In retrospect, Mrs Jones agreed that this was more or less the opposite of what she had done before. Previously, he had gained her attention by his inappropriate behaviour, and as soon as she had settled him back to work, she had busied herself with the other pupils who were trying to work, yet needed help and encouragement.

It must also be pointed out that Mrs Jones didn't find the treatment particularly easy to apply. When first advised to ignore Frank's inappropriate behaviour as much as possible, she did have some misgivings. She also found it difficult at first to catch him working, and so give him attention. These difficulties were exacerbated by the fact that when she began to apply the technique, Frank's inappropriate behaviour increased a little before it settled into a steady decline. However, Mrs Jones persevered with the treatment and after four weeks she was pleased with the results.

Recording a pupil's behaviour for ten minutes a day throughout six weeks may seem to be an unusual procedure. However, it does give a baseline against which to evaluate treatment, and it supplies an indication of progress, or lack of progress if that be the case. It is a safeguard against not noticing small changes in behaviour, and it helps to focus attention on behaviours of concern.

There are many pupils like Frank in classrooms, and indeed some teachers feel from time to time that all their pupils are like this. However, for Mrs Jones, Frank's behaviour was a problem, and this is how she reduced the problem.

Tom

Tom was a pupil in a special school for pupils with moderate learning difficulties [ESN(M)]. He was aged fourteen. He had a measured I.Q. of 74, reading age of 7.6, and an arithmetic age of 6.9. When the class were supposed to be working, he would frequently talk with other pupils, speak out to the teacher, cough very loudly, ignore the teacher, and take a walk around the classroom. These behaviours were very disruptive.

Tom's teacher, Mr Brown, classified these disruptive behaviours into the following categories:

1 talking to other pupils;
2 speaking out to the teacher when this was not required; coughing loudly;
3 ignoring the teacher;
4 being out of his seat when he ought to be in it working.

In order to gain an estimate of how frequently these behaviours occurred, Mr Brown continued to teach in his normal way, and noted the incidence of the behaviours when the class was meant to be working. Like Mrs Jones, the previous teacher, he took a time sample of his pupil's behaviour. Mr Brown took his time sample at the same part of the same kind of lesson twice a week for four weeks.

In addition to obtaining this estimate of Tom's inappropriate behaviours in class, Mr Brown was also aware that Tom bullied other pupils, and gave cheek to other members of staff, including the ladies who worked in the school dining room. In addition, he frequently arrived late for school.

Mr Brown spent a lesson with the class discussing the rules of the classroom, and included in this lesson some discussion about the problems raised by talking to other pupils, speaking out when not required to, coughing loudly, ignoring the teacher, and pupils being out of the seat when they were supposed to be working. Specific reference was not made to Tom.

Following this, Mr Brown had a lengthy private discussion with Tom. He explained that he felt Tom's behaviour was neither helping Tom nor the class, and said that he wanted to help Tom to improve. After a brief negotiation, a contract was drawn up between Mr Brown and Tom. It was as follows:

1 During each number lesson, Tom had to complete fifteen sums or ten problems, whichever were set. During each language lesson, Tom had to produce at least 150 written words or answer ten questions from a comprehension book. If he kept to this schedule, he would be allowed to play

badminton, which he enjoyed, at lunch time on Mondays and Thursdays.

2. For one month, Tom was not to bully other pupils or to give cheek to any member of the school staff, including the dinner ladies. For this, he would be allowed to go with a school party to a weekend camp. For two months of such good conduct, he would be allowed to go to the school camp for a week.
3. If Tom was late for school, he had to make up for any work missed before he could play badminton.
4. Mr Brown was to increase his rate of praise whenever Tom was behaving well.

In addition to these contingencies agreed with Tom, Mr Brown decided to minimize his attention to Tom when he was not behaving well.

The contract was in operation for five weeks, until the end of the term, and Mr Brown continued to take his twice-weekly observations of Tom's behaviour. During this time, Tom's inappropriate behaviours decreased by 34 per cent, his punctuality increased, he ceased to bully other pupils, and he stopped giving cheek to other members of staff. Tom earned his camping trip.

COMMENT This case was of a different order from the previous one. The behaviours were more serious, when one considers Tom's age, and his 'out of class' activities. Mr Brown had previously used 'rules, attention and ignoring' successfully with other pupils, but had found little success when applying these techniques with Tom. In Tom, he felt he had a pupil who didn't find his teacher's attention to be rewarding. That being the case, he had to find what was rewarding to Tom, and how the school could reward Tom for appropriate behaviour.

As the contract indicates, Mr Brown knew Tom to be interested in badminton and camping. Generally, pupils like Tom, whose behaviour was poor, had little opportunity to take part in these activities. The contract gave Tom his opportunity.

The fourth point in the contract, that is that Mr Brown was to increase his rate of praise whenever Tom was behaving well, may seem a little unnecessary. However, this was a very important feature of the contract; from Tom's viewpoint, it was a signal to tell him that he was fulfilling the contract, from Mr Brown's point of view, it was an attempt to give a rewarding value to his praise and attention to Tom's good work. Since Mr Brown was also involved in organizing and running the school camp, and was in charge of the sporting facilities in the school, there were further opportunities for Tom to find Mr Brown's attention rewarding.

The formal contract ended when the term finished for the Easter holidays. At the start of the final term of the school year, Mr Brown felt that Tom was behaving sufficiently well to be treated in the same way as the rest of the class, without a contract. Tom had no special treatment during this term, and his behaviour continued to improve.

Billy

Billy was a comprehensive school pupil aged thirteen. He was above average in ability, but had come to the school with a record of behaviour problems in his three primary schools. Because of his disruptive behaviour in the comprehensive school, he was put into a special class along with five other pupils who were unable to adjust to normal classroom conditions. The pupils took most of their lessons in this classroom with their teacher, Mr Davies.

After three months in the class, it became apparent to Mr Davies that Billy needed special treatment. He had become the class leader, and tended to instigate misbehaviour. He would frequently make comments of a provocative nature, and from time to time would roam restlessly about the classroom when he was supposed to be working. These two categories of behaviour were selected by Mr Davies for observation.

Over a period of three weeks, Mr Davies unobtrusively observed Billy for fifteen minutes per day, when work ought to have been taking place. This gave the baseline estimate.

After this, Mr Davies and Billy were called to a meeting with the school's deputy headmaster, who explained that because of his intelligence, Billy had been selected to record in a 'class log book', the day-to-day events in the special class. The purpose of the log book was to explain what was happening in the class, which was experimental, to the deputy headmaster, to the headmaster, and to visitors who were interested. The deputy headmaster made it clear that keeping the log book was a privilege to be safeguarded by good behaviour.

Mr Davies then explained the purpose of the class to Billy, and made a contract with him. It was pointed out to Billy that his comments were not helpful, and that roaming about the classroom was not the best way to behave. It was agreed that Mr Davies would sign Billy's exercise book after each ten-minute period in which these behaviours did not occur. Whenever four signatures had been accumulated, Billy could fill in the log book if he so wished. At the end of each session, Billy was to take the log book to the deputy headmaster, who would read it with considerable interest.

When the contract was implemented, Mr Davies continued to take his fifteen-minute observations of Billy's behaviour.

After a number of lessons, Billy often chose not to fill in the log book at the permitted times, and instead, took it home to complete. The incidence of his inappropriate behaviours dropped dramatically, from an average of five per fifteen minutes observation to an average of less than once per fifteen minutes.

After less than three weeks of 'log keeping', Mr Davies judged that Billy no longer needed observing. He also agreed with Billy that the signatures were a waste of time, and that Billy could keep on with the log book as long as he behaved well.

Generally, the whole class improved. Mr Davies noted a higher standard of work from the pupils, a more restrained attitude to informal work, and a more relaxed and accepting attitude between the pupils.

COMMENT There are a number of interesting features in this investigation. The treatment worked dramatically, although it took a long time to devise it. Mr Davies was taking part in an in-service course for teachers in behaviour modification when he was deciding upon the treatment. He was able to draw on the experience of ten teachers and two psychologists before making his decision.

The problems Mr Davies faced were not restricted to Billy's behaviour. The class was by no means easy to teach. However, by taking the class leader as his subject, and improving his behaviour, Mr Davies was able to alleviate the problems posed by the class.

When deciding upon the kind of treatment to be used, the key consideration was Billy's desire to be treated as an adult, a not uncommon characteristic of pupils of his age. At the same time, Mr Davies knew that Billy had a great deal of respect for the deputy headmaster. By keeping the log book, Billy was allowed to act responsibly, and by taking it to the deputy headmaster, he was being rewarded for his responsible behaviour.

Initially the treatment appeared to be very artificial, and Mr Davies had to remember to sign Billy's book every ten minutes. At the start of the treatment, there was some concern over how this might be faded out; for example, could the time gradually be increased to half an hour? In practice, there was no need to worry. It rapidly became evident that the signatures were redundant.

Peter

Peter was an infant school pupil aged six. He was above average in intelligence and physically very mature for his age. He was bigger and stronger than the other pupils in the class, and he used his physique quite forcibly at times. In general, he would behave well in class, and he would rapidly become absorbed in whatever he was doing. He worked well and played happily with the other pupils. However, his teacher, Mrs Evans, was very concerned about Peter's inability to queue properly.

Whenever the class had to line up for any reason, Peter shot to the front. If any one else was there before him, he 'bounced' him or her right out of the line. This behaviour wasn't taken lightly by some of the pupils, nor by Mrs Evans. Nevertheless, the behaviour continued.

To obtain a measure of the incidence of this behaviour, Mrs Evans decided to count how often it occurred each day. Over a period of two weeks, every time the class lined up, Peter dashed to the front. Whenever he was beaten for the position, he 'bounced' the other pupil out.

Treatment for this behaviour was done in two situations, the first when the class was lining up to leave the classroom, and the second during P.E. lessons.

When the class was about to be lined up, Mrs Evans would engage Peter in conversation, usually about his work, and at the same time, keep a restraining hand on his shoulder. Still talking with him, she would ease him into the line, near, but not at the front.

P.E. was a more difficult problem, since there was potential danger in Peter's behaviour when the pupils were using apparatus in turns. To combat this, Mrs Evans used a 'musical chairs' technique. The apparatus used by Peter's group was strung out, and the number in the group reduced, so that by the time Peter had moved around the apparatus and arrived back at the start, the last pupil had moved off. As Peter came back to the start, Mrs Evans would greet him with encouraging comments about his performance. He rapidly became used to this routine. Gradually, over a period of several P.E. lessons, Mrs Evans decreased the range of apparatus, until Peter was arriving at the start with one or more pupils waiting in front of him. She continued to be there and comment on his performance. Peter didn't push the other pupils out. He slowed down and waited for comments. At this point, Mrs Evans began to worry that he might stand still and wave the others on! To her relief, he didn't do this.

As Peter's behaviour began to improve, so Mrs Evans began to forget occasionally to reach him at the appropriate times. Even so, he did not revert to his original behaviour.

COMMENT The reward used with Peter is in complete contrast with the rewards used in the two previous cases, with older pupils. This case illustrates how, in general terms, a class teacher can be rewarding to a younger pupil by giving her attention at the appropriate time.

The treatment began to fade out naturally. In practice, once a behaviour has been developed by being continually rewarded, it is best maintained by frequent, but not continuous reward. Consequently, whilst a teacher needs to be very consistent initially, this consistency has to be relaxed in the later stages of treatment. Very often, this relaxation occurs quite naturally, as happened in this case.

It is worth noting that Peter's behaviour was recorded by a simple count, rather than by a time sample. If behaviour is infrequent, then a simple count is the better of the two methods. Additionally, it will have been noted that Mrs Evans obtained a very stable baseline measure of Peter's 'bouncing' behaviour. No averages needed to be reported.

Jane

Jane was a pupil in a school for maladjusted children. She was twelve years old. According to her teacher, Mrs Green, she had a number of problems. Jane had a very poor relationship with the other pupils; when she wasn't being 'picked on', she was being aggressive. She had a hearing deficiency, and for a while it had been very difficult to persuade her to wear the hearing aid which had been prescribed for her. Jane did very little work in school.

Mrs Green felt that she was making social progress with Jane, but was very concerned by the lack of academic progress. When work was set for the class, Jane would often go into a kind of trance. In Mrs Green's words, 'she switched off'. She would gaze into space, avoiding eye contact. She wouldn't acknowledge words spoken to her by Mrs Green, or by other pupils. Even when she was spoken to from six inches in front of her face, she sometimes didn't appear to notice.

Mrs Green decided to measure the incidence of 'switching off', and counted the number of times it occurred each day for a week. However, significantly, whilst she was obtaining this baseline estimate, Mrs Green noticed that 'switching off' invariably began when the pupils were meant to start working.

Mrs Green treated the behaviour by arranging to be with Jane when the work was being set, and giving attention to her as work was begun. Whilst Jane was working, Mrs Green gave her as much attention as was possible.

This treatment was very successful. 'Switching off', which occurred some three or four times a day during the baseline recording, did not occur when Mrs Green followed the treatment procedure. However, Mrs Green did experience difficulty when she tried to fade out the treatment. Attention had to be withdrawn very gradually if the behaviour was not to recur.

Despite this difficulty, Jane's output of work increased considerably. She usually completed the work set, and Mrs Green was able to put good comments on her books. Jane began to take more interest in her work.

COMMENT This case was included for a number of reasons. 'Switching off' is a most unusual problem, but one can make a good guess at how this developed by looking at the case history. Before Jane wore the hearing aid, she may well have had many experiences of not hearing what work was being set. Under such circumstances, sitting deep in thought is not an unusual response. When she was given a hearing aid, she would have heard more demands being made upon her. One can understand her reluctance to wear the aid. However, given that she had to wear the aid, a way out of the demands would be not to hear the instructions. If a sympathetic teacher accepted that Jane 'switched off' from time to time, this behaviour could have been inadvertently rewarded.

Before obtaining a baseline measure of the incidence of the behaviour, Mrs Green had not really noticed precisely when the behaviour occurred. However, whilst taking the observations, she noticed that the behaviour always began when work was set. One may wonder why Mrs Green hadn't noticed this before. There are at least two reasons for this. First, Mrs Green did have her other pupils to consider, and it isn't always easy to see the idiosyncrasies of one pupil when others are requiring attention; secondly, Jane didn't always 'switch off'. Sometimes she would start to work at the same time as the others, and continue working.

A final point on this case concerns the fading out of the treatment. In many cases, as indicated previously, this can occur even without conscious planning. Mrs Green, on the other hand, had to work very hard to fade the treatment, and had to find out by trial and error how and when to diminish the treatment that Jane was receiving.

Teddy

Teddy was a primary school pupil aged ten. He was in the remedial class, and had been there for two years. Teddy's reading age was 8.5, and this was higher than most of the class. However, his work output in the English lessons was the lowest in the class. His handwriting was clear but laboured, and his work was characterised by retracing and 'doodling'.

There was a reward system operating in the school. The pupils could earn points for good work. If sufficient points were accumulated, they could be exchanged for a half-hour session of badminton, table tennis, or snooker after school. This system seemed to work well with the majority of the pupils. However, Teddy was one of the two pupils out of 76 children involved who had never accumulated sufficient points to attend the session.

Teddy's teacher, Mr Morris, was understandably worried about the disparity between Teddy's ability and his work output.

Each day from 11 a.m. to 12 noon, the pupils worked from an English book, doing exercises. To gain a point, pupils were required to complete three exercises, which involved putting approximately 100 words on paper. During two weeks of observation, Teddy averaged 29 words in this hour.

It was decided that the best way to tackle this low work rate would be to arrange that Teddy could obtain the reward at least once, without too much effort. Once he had enjoyed the half-hour session, it ought to be possible to increase what was required of him.

A confidential arrangement was made with Teddy. He would be given a point whenever he wrote 50 words in the hour. On the first day after the arrangement, he produced 54 words, but on subsequent days his output fell below 50. On the last two days of the week he wrote 21 and 28 words. At the end of the week, the treatment was discontinued. The reward system seemed to be ineffective with Teddy.

Following this, Mr Morris chatted with Teddy to try and find out just what interested him. This revealed that Teddy was very interested in collecting model cars. Consequently, a new arrangement was made. It was agreed that Teddy could earn a car by completing 50 words or more in each of ten lessons, although the lessons did not have to be consecutive.

During the next ten lessons, Teddy averaged 108 words, and received his car.

Following this success, the same arrangement was made again, and for a further five lessons, Teddy's output increased to an average of 121 words.

At this point, Teddy left the school. His father had obtained a job abroad, and the school had been unaware of Teddy's impending departure.

COMMENT The results of the treatment showed that Mr Morris's initial worry about Teddy's work output was justified. Teddy was averaging 29 words an hour before the treatment, and by the end of the treatment he was averaging 121 words an hour.

The first attempt at treating Teddy, using the pre-existing reward system, proved to be unsuccessful. This sometimes happens in behaviour modification investigations. It is never known precisely whether a treatment will be effective or not, and there is only one way to find out.

The treatment which was effective does however raise a more fundamental question. Teddy might well have produced even more words if he had been promised a transistor radio for increasing his output. Yet, given the aim that the special treatment would eventually be faded out, and bearing in mind the functioning of the school system, such a treatment would hardly be realistic. If a teacher judges that mere social rewards are ineffective, and that he needs to introduce a new reward-system, he must strive to find a reward which is effective, yet is as little different as possible from the normal reward system being used in the school. This is why it is sometimes necessary to try out more than one treatment, whilst slowly moving along a continuum away from social rewards towards more intrusive rewards, that is, towards rewards which differ from those normally in use.

The reward used in the successful treatment, model cars, may well raise uneasy thoughts in the minds of some readers. Occasionally, the accusation of 'bribery' is levelled at the use of such rewards. Let us examine this. The *Concise Oxford Dictionary* (1975) defines 'to bribe' as, 'to pervert by gifts or other inducements the action or judgement of'. To pervert is defined in terms of leading astray. Even allowing for the fact that a close association with the use of behaviour modification techniques has biased the writer's views, it does not seem possible to reconcile the treatment of Teddy, and the results obtained, with the way in which bribery is defined. There are of course, additional philosophical questions raised here, and these will be discussed in Chapter 7.

The measure used in evaluating the treatment was concerned with academic performance. This is very different from the other cases previously discussed. There was also an element of comparison with other pupils indicated, that is, the other pupils gained a point when they wrote 100 words in an hour. This kind of comparison was not explicitly made in the other cases, but this is not to say that it wasn't present in the teachers' minds. Whilst certain pupil behaviours are labelled 'inappropriate' by teachers, very often it is not so much the performance of these behaviours as their frequency which is important. A pupil who continually interrupts his neighbour by chatting is behaving inappropriately. However, if he chats occasionally to his neighbour, this may be quite appropriate. This may well be the way in which other pupils behave, and the teacher may feel that this is part of a good, relaxed working atmosphere.

Joe

Joe was a comprehensive school pupil aged thirteen. He was in a normal class, but had previously been in a special unit for disruptive pupils. Mr Johnson, who took the class for English, expressed his concern about Joe's behaviour in class. Joe would (a) call out answers without raising his hand, (b) call out irrelevant comments, (c) talk with other pupils, (d) mutter loudly to himself. These behaviours were interfering with learning during the English lessons.

To obtain a baseline estimate of these behaviours, Joe was observed during his English lessons with Mr Johnson over a two-week period of time. Two student-teachers sitting in with the class did the observing.

When the baseline period had been completed, Mr Johnson talked with Joe. He told Joe that he had been keeping a note of his behaviour, and listed the four behaviours which were of concern. He indicated his desire to help Joe do better in class, and asked him to keep a record of his own behaviour. Mr Johnson explained to Joe that he needed the record to see if there really was a problem.

At the start of each English lesson, Joe was given a sheet of paper on which he had to fill in the lesson number, the date, and a record of the number of times he had behaved inappropriately during the lesson. There was also a space on the sheet where Mr Johnson was to mark in the number of inappropriate behaviours he noted. At the end of each lesson, Joe was to sign the sheet, indicating that he had filled it in honestly, and hand it back to Mr Johnson.

This procedure was put into practice and continued for two weeks. During this time, the student teachers continued to observe. The results obtained by the observers, showed that Joe's inappropriate behaviours decreased during the last five lessons in which Joe recorded his own behaviour to 25 per cent of the baseline level.

Self-recording continued for a further four weeks without the student observers being present. Finally, self-recording was discontinued, and Joe's behaviour was again observed by the student teachers for three more lessons. In these three lessons the inappropriate behaviours rose a little, but remained at 50 per cent below the baseline level.

On the other hand, whilst Mr Johnson and the observers noted that there was a marked decrease in Joe's inappropriate behaviours, the small amount that remained consisted almost entirely of the disruptive element, 'calling out'. In addition, there was an increase in other inappropriate behaviours; for example, on several occasions, Joe threw objects at classmates merely to attract their attention, whereas when not on self-recording, he would have shouted at them.

Despite this cautionary note, Mr Johnson was pleased with the results. He felt that Joe was working better in class, and that he was thinking about questions before raising his hand. Both Mr Johnson and the observers found Joe's self-recording to be completely honest.

COMMENT This case was included because it does show a different way in which behaviour modification principles have been applied. The pupil was treated by being required to observe his own behaviour. This is not the place to discuss the theory behind self-recording, but, very briefly, the idea is that pupils ought to be given responsibility in regulating their own behaviour, that is, to develop self-control. Aspects of this which have been investigated include self-recording, self-evaluation and self-reward. There will be further discussion of these in subsequent chapters.

In the previous cases, the teacher has been the observer. In this case, independent observers were introduced into the classroom. This procedure has advantages and disadvantages, and these will be explored later in the text. The immediate advantage in this investigation was that the observers could record for long periods of time in any one lesson. This would have been impossible for the teacher to do. Consequently, for those lessons during which the observers recorded, a detailed measure of Joe's behaviour was obtained. The immediate disadvantage for this investigation, was that the observers, who were student teachers, were not available for an unlimited time. Whilst the experience of observing was undoubtedly beneficial to their teacher-training, there were other demands on their time. This accounts for the comparative brevity of the investigation.

Another way in which this case differs from those discussed previously is in the amount of contact the teacher had with his pupil. This was a secondary school, and Mr Johnson only took the class for English lessons. This occasional contact which a secondary school teacher has with his pupils is one of the current problems which behaviour modification faces. When a pupil is taught by up to seven or eight teachers in one day, consistency of treatment is very difficult to achieve. Because of this, self-recording, across a series of lessons, may prove to be beneficial.

Arthur

Arthur was a primary school pupil aged nine. He was a very diligent worker and was of average ability in most subjects. He was very good at Art.

Arthur did not have any behaviours which concerned his teacher, Mr Edwards. What did concern Mr Edwards was the behaviours which Arthur lacked. Arthur never seemed to be involved in any form of social contact. He didn't ask questions, he seldom seemed to speak with the other pupils, and he responded to questions with one- or two-word answers. It was almost as if he wasn't part of the class.

Mr Edwards felt that Arthur did want to join in, but that he didn't know how to make contact. Any attempts at contact seemed to make Arthur nervous and he would withdraw into silence.

In order to obtain a measure of Arthur's behaviour, Mr Edwards noted the number of times he spoke in class during each day for a week. The results showed that he spoke an average of five or six times a day. He took the initiative once during Art, when he borrowed a rubber from another pupil, but all the other talk from Arthur was in response to someone else. Not once did he say more than two or three words.

Initially, Mr Edwards decided that he ought to get to know Arthur better. He talked to him on his own, and found that, after some initial hesitancy, Arthur began to talk more. However, Mr Edwards found that this wouldn't generalize to normal classroom conditions. Arthur would still not say more than two or three words in class, nor would he initiate talking.

Following this unsuccessful attempt at getting Arthur involved,

Mr Edwards decided to try a different strategy. The class were to produce a huge painting depicting 'The Romans in Britain', to be displayed in the school entrance hall. Different groups of pupils within the class were given different parts on which to concentrate. Arthur and another boy, John, who was good at Art, were given the task of drawing in the people. This meant that they had to move about the groups responding to demand. John revelled in this task, and tended to become a little bossy and dictatorial. Arthur, on the other hand, performed quietly and soberly, and did what was required of him.

Over the course of several lessons, Mr Edwards noticed that Arthur was becoming more involved. The pupils he worked with began to ask his advice on where to place the people, what the people should be doing, how buildings could best be drawn, and so on. Arthur began to respond and he talked.

During these lessons, Mr Edwards would circulate around the groups to offer his advice, and to give praise and encouragement to the pupils.

In the ordinary lessons, Arthur began to talk more often. He continued to be a responder rather than an initiator of talk, and he still gave very short replies. However, he did become more involved with the other pupils.

When Mr Edwards watched Arthur's behaviour again for a week, he noted that Arthur was talking at more than double his former frequency during ordinary lessons. During Art lessons he was talking almost continually.

COMMENT This case was included because it illustrates a kind of difficulty not frequently discussed in behaviour modification investigations. Pupils who are 'withdrawn' can slip by unnoticed in classrooms. They do not disrupt the general tenor of the lessons, and their lack of certain behaviours inconveniences no one but themselves. True, there are some pupils whose isolation seems to be self-selected, and these are often very self-sufficient individuals. On the other hand, there are some pupils who wish to mix and yet seem unable to do so. Teachers can usually differentiate between these two kinds of pupil.

The case illustrates once again that an initial method of treatment may be ineffective. Arthur would talk with Mr Edwards when alone, but not in class. Talking to Mr Edwards would not generalize from one situation to another.

When Mr Edwards decided to use the Art lessons as a form of treatment, he placed Arthur in what is sometimes called a 'behavioural trap'. Arthur's ability in Art produced initiations from the other pupils. He was able to respond in a way which rewarded them. This increased the initiations from the other pupils, and so the pattern of interactions continued. This behaviour did generalize to ordinary classroom lessons.

Some Unusual Consequences

So far, eight cases have been discussed. These have all differed quite considerably along a number of dimensions. However, they have all been relatively straightforward cases, and in perusing these alone, the reader could be misled into believing that behaviour modification invariably produces such results. This isn't always so. In order to give a more complete picture, some unusual consequences are presented here.

The Vanishing Problem

This is a feature which sometimes occurs when a teacher sets out to obtain a baseline estimate of a pupil's behaviour. The teacher defines the problem, sets up categories of behaviour to observe, and begins to record, only to find the problem doesn't exist. Inappropriate behaviour vanishes and appropriate behaviour emerges. Exactly what happens isn't really clear, but it seems likely that the pupil responds to a change in the teacher's behaviour. This phenomenon has been the subject of some discussion (Harrop, 1977b), and it has been estimated that vanishing problems occur in some 14 per cent of cases treated in ordinary schools.

Without prior warning, teachers can become discouraged when a problem vanishes just as they are about to begin an investigation. However, whilst a vanishing problem may be disconcerting, it ought to be kept in mind that it does involve a very efficient, if mysterious, form of treatment.

Ignoring a Pupil's Behaviour

A number of classroom behaviour modification investigations rely for treatment upon a combination of emphasizing classroom rules, giving attention for appropriate behaviour and ignoring inappropriate behaviour. Of these three teacher behaviours, the one which causes the most difficulty is ignoring. Very often teachers don't like to do this. It conflicts with their usual practice.

The crux of the difficulty seems to lie in how much to ignore. If ignoring is taken to its extreme, there is a danger of escalation. Harrop and McNamara (1979) describe such a case, in which a pupil's behaviour changed from 'fiddling with an object beneath the desk' to 'cartwheeling across the classroom floor'. Sometimes, of course, a pupil's inappropriate behaviour is rewarded by the reactions of his classmates. There are a number of ways in which this may be dealt with. It may be that a simple alteration of seating arrangements will reduce inappropriate behaviour, and a good indication of the effectiveness of this is seen in the work of Wheldall *et al* (1981), who found that seating fourth year junior school pupils in rows rather than around tables, increased the 'on-task' behaviour of the pupils. Moreover, it was the pupils who spent least time 'on-task' when seated at tables who showed the most increase when they were seated in rows. Alternatively, it may be that the teacher arranges to treat the whole class, as is seen in the work of Tsoi and Yule (1976) and Merrett and Wheldall (1978). This is discussed further in Chapter 6.

Allied to the problem of escalation is the problem of contagion (Clarizio and Yelon, 1976). If the inappropriate behaviour of one pupil is too obviously ignored, the other pupils in the class may infer that the rules of the classroom can be ignored, and this may produce unfortunate consequences.

Finally, there is the problem of dangerous behaviour, and this cannot be ignored.

The Storm before the Calm

This feature was mentioned briefly when discussing the first case, the treatment of Frank. His teacher noticed that when she treated him, his inappropriate behaviour increased a little, before decreasing. This is a very common initial response to treatment, and it can be very worrying for a teacher.

A simple analogy illustrates how this may occur. We have learned that turning a door knob and pulling or pushing normally results in the door opening. We are rewarded by being able to pass through the doorway. Yet suppose the door is locked without our knowing. What do we do? We are liable to exert more pressure, and try various kinds of behaviour, until we are convinced that we are not going to open the door without the key.

The pupil who is being treated is in a similar position. He finds the behaviour which previous gained reward is ineffective. In these circumstances, he may redouble his efforts in an attempt to gain reward. At this time, the teacher needs to be as consistent as the locked door, and the pupil needs to learn that the 'key' to gaining rewards lies in behaving appropriately. This may well take a little time.

Further Comments

By this stage, the reader should have a good general picture of the applications of behaviour modification in the classroom, and an appreciation of many of the decisions which have to be made when treating a pupil. In order to put this knowledge into a proper perspective, let us now look briefly at these decisions in the order in which they have to be taken by the teacher.

Inevitably, the first decision is concerned with what constitutes inappropriate behaviour in the classroom. This isn't the kind of question which can be answered by drawing up a list. What is inappropriate in one setting might be quite appropriate in another, and vice-versa. A useful way of making this decision is to look for behaviour which interferes with the pupil's own learning, and which may also interfere with the learning of others. Such behaviour is inappropriate. The kind of pupil who immediately springs to mind when using such criteria is the one who is out-going and causes some disruption. However, there are pupils like Arthur, whose case has just been discussed, who are not disruptive. Their inappropriate behaviour includes, 'not attending, not joining in activities, not asking for help when it is needed' and so on, and this does not interfere with the learning of other pupils. Such pupils need sympathetic help.

When inappropriate behaviour has been identified, it needs to be defined and measured before any treatment is applied, and it should be emphasized at this point that whilst the word 'treatment' may have different connotations, it is used in this text with specific reference to behaviour modification procedures. The pre-treatment measure gives a baseline estimate against which the effects of treatment can be evaluated. How to measure the behaviours of concern depends upon such factors as their frequency, and the times at which they occur. If a particular behaviour is relatively infrequent then a simple count during the day, or lesson, can be made. If, however, the behaviour is very frequent, then the teacher must take a time sample at pre-set intervals.

Quite naturally, teachers do not wish to take very lengthy baselines, since they are eager to treat the behaviours of concern. However, if a baseline shows very irregular rates of behaviour, then it really ought to be prolonged a little in the hope that the behaviour 'steadies down'. Occasionally, the baseline itself will indicate a steady improvement, in which case it might be wise to continue with baseline observations to see if the problem vanishes. Should the baseline show a steady deterioration in behaviour, then treatment ought to be brought forward.

Deciding upon a form of treatment involves a careful analysis of what is occurring in the classroom. This means that a close examination must be made of the pupil's behaviour, and of the rewards this obtains. Every case is of course, unique, so that, here, a firm grasp of the principles of behaviour modification is essential, together with a good knowledge of what has been done by teachers in similar situations. In addition, the characteristics and background of the pupil concerned must be borne in mind. For example, it would not be good practice to remove attention from a pupil who is known to be starved of affection at home. With such a pupil, the treatment ought to involve giving him more attention, but at appropriate times.

One aspect of treatment as yet not discussed is the curriculum material being used. The assumption is usually made that the teacher has examined this aspect of the problem before selecting a pupil for treatment. However, it needs to be emphasized that if each pupil found the material with which he was working to be very enjoyable, there would be few behaviour problems. From an educational standpoint of course, this material must not only be enjoyable, but must also meet the learning requirements of the pupil. Here is the rub. The teacher, with limited financial resources at his disposal must continually seek for such material to suit the needs of each one of his pupils. Whilst behaviour modification techniques can alleviate the difficulties faced by the teacher, they must not be allowed to supplant this fundamental educational duty. The use of behaviour modification to 'prop up' an inadequate curriculum would truly be perversion.

When treatment begins, the aim is to increase appropriate behaviour and decrease inappropriate behaviour. This is when the teacher has to be very consistent in rewarding what is appropriate and minimising rewards to the inappropriate. It can be difficult to catch some pupils behaving appropriately and great vigilance needs to be maintained. At the same time, it needs to be kept in mind that the pupil may show some deterioriation in behaviour before improving. Differentiating this from a treatment which is having a deleterious effect requires careful judgement.

If it is the considered opinion of the teacher and of the appropriate authorities that the pupil really belongs in the class, then the treatment decided upon ought to include a way in which treatment can be 'faded out'. This is because the ultimate aim must be that the pupil functions in the same way as the rest of the pupils. For this reason, social reward, using teacher attention, should be the first treatment considered. If this is thought to be unrealistic, then more 'powerful' rewards may have to be considered, even though they are more intrusive. However, these ought always to be paired with teacher approval, with the aim that teacher approval will itself become rewarding.

When treatment is applied, recording must continue exactly as before, so that the results of treatment can be observed and evaluated.

The fading out of a treatment can sometimes occur quite naturally, as indicated earlier. In other cases, it can take a good deal of effort. The power of occasional but frequent rewards can be a great advantage at this juncture. When once a behaviour has been established by continually being rewarded, it is maintained most strongly by occasional rewards. This is undoubtedly why many inappropriate behaviours are so intractable. They are being maintained by occasional rewards. The message is clear. Once the pupil is behaving appropriately and being consistently rewarded, steps must be taken to reduce the frequency of the reward.

In the long term, the final evaluation ought to indicate that the pupil behaves in the same way as the rest of the class, under the influence of the same rewards. This outcome may not be achieved given the time at the teacher's disposal, but it should always remain the final goal.

In Conclusion

The aim of this chapter has been to demonstrate that behaviour modification is a practical approach to some of the problems which concern teachers. This has been attempted by examining a series of situations in which teachers have treated pupils in their own classrooms, and drawing from these cases some of the fundamental considerations involved. In some of the cases the treatment has been relatively straightforward, in others, considerable ingenuity has been demonstrated.

In order to achieve the aim of the chapter, it has been necessary to postpone a full discussion of many aspects of behaviour modification to subsequent chapters, and to ignore for the present the traditional ways in which schools allocate their rewards and punishments. Many questions will have occurred to the reader by now, and it is hoped that the answers to these questions will be found further along in the book.

Chapter 2

The Theory and Basic Procedures of Behaviour Modification

The cases which were described in the previous chapter illustrate how behaviour modification techniques may be used by teachers to help pupils overcome various difficulties. Each case was followed by a brief comment which indicated some of the more important features of the procedure used. The combination of cases followed by comments should have given the reader a basic grasp of the way in which behaviour modification can be applied. The aim of this chapter is to extend that basic grasp into a deeper understanding of the fundamentals of behaviour modification.

To Set the Record Straight

Behaviour modifiers are frequently accused of neglecting the curriculum, and of spending their time concentrating on rewards which are external to the learning task. In a sense, this is a valid criticism. If books and articles written by behaviour modifiers are examined, little or no comment is generally found on the curriculum. This is an unfortunate omission, and because of the importance of the curriculum material it is necessary to re-emphasize that the use of other procedures should be delayed until the curriculum has been carefully examined.

If the development of behaviour modification is traced back, it is found that the research and writing of B. F. Skinner has had a considerable influence. In 1968, he wrote *The Technology of Teaching*, attacking aversive control, and pointing to the relative infrequency of the use of rewards in schools. At the same time however, he very clearly pointed to an examination of the curriculum. Consider these quotations from his book.

'What does the school have in its possession which will reinforce (reward) a child? We may look first to the material to be learned, for it is possible that this will provide considerable automatic reinforcement. Children will play for hours with mechanical toys, paints, scissors and paper, noise-makers, puzzles – in short, with almost anything which feeds back significant changes in the environment and is reasonably free of aversive properties.'

'If natural reinforcement inherent in the subject matter is not enough, other reinforcers must be employed.'

These are very clear statements of the order in which the behaviour modifier ought to proceed; that is, he should seek to make the curriculum rewarding before considering other rewards. Why then do behaviour modifiers discuss the curriculum so infrequently when they report their investigations? There are at least three possible answers to this question:

1 An examination of the curriculum was undertaken before procedures external to the task were considered, and this earlier stage remained unreported because it did not solve the pupil's difficulties.
2 An examination of the curriculum material revealed a solution to the pupil's difficulties, and this was unreported because it was a normal teaching process.
3 The pupil's difficulties were social, and as such were considered to be unrelated to the curriculum.

In the second quotation, Skinner recognizes that the teacher may not always be successful in his search for appropriate curriculum material. That this should sometimes be the case is inevitable, when one appreciates the differences of background and abilities that pupils bring to the learning task, and the limited resources of time and money at the teacher's disposal. However, whilst the teacher may not always be successful in his search for appropriate curriculum materials, this is a task which must always be in the forefront of his thinking.

Reward and Punishment

We all know what we mean by the words 'reward' and 'punishment'. And indeed, the word 'reward' was used extensively in the previous chapter when the various cases were discussed. However, if a teacher decides to reward a pupil for good behaviour, it is not sufficient to apply the reward and then assume the pupil will behave well. Unless the pupil's behaviour is systematically observed both before and after the reward is applied, the teacher can only speculate on the effectiveness of the reward.

To say that a reward can be ineffective sounds like a contradiction. However, what the teacher thinks the pupil will find rewarding, may not be what the pupil does find rewarding. This shows the confusion that the use of the word reward can generate. The same problem exists with the word punishment. If a teacher punishes a pupil for an unwanted behaviour, and the behaviour continues, has the pupil been punished? The teacher feels sure the pupil has been punished, yet the punishment seems to have acted as a reward.

In order to avoid becoming involved in this kind of tortuous reasoning, behaviour modifiers have developed their own terms which are rather more specific and depend upon behavioural consequences. Instead of talking about rewards and punishments, they talk about reinforcers.

Reinforcers

A reinforcer is an event which increases or maintains the rate of a prior behaviour.

Consider a pupil who is trying to complete a difficult task. He looks at his teacher who nods and smiles reassuringly. If the pupil continues with the task, he has been reinforced. The nod and smile from the teacher have acted as a reinforcer for the pupil's behaviour. Had the pupil given up the task, the nod and smile would not have been a reinforcer for the behaviour.

In this example, the teacher reinforced the behaviour by presenting something, nodding and smiling. It is also possible to reinforce a behaviour by removing something.

Consider now the same pupil, who, in the presence of his teacher, is struggling to complete a gymnastic exercise. Sensing the pupil's embarrassment, the teacher moves away and gives his attention to other pupils. In the absence of the teacher, the pupil works more efficiently at the gymnastics.

Here, it is the removal of the teacher's attention which has reinforced the behaviour.

Because it is possible to reinforce behaviour either by presenting something, or by removing something, we have two kinds of reinforcers, and these are known as positive reinforcers and negative reinforcers respectively. To put it more clearly:

> *A positive reinforcer* is one which, when presented, maintains or increases the rate of a prior behaviour.
>
> *A negative reinforcer* is one which, when removed, maintains or increases the rate of a prior behaviour.

Whilst the definitions of positive and negative reinforcers look comparatively straightforward, it is appreciated that these are not the simplest of concepts to understand, and two further examples may help clarify the definitions. When a teacher increases a pupil's work rate by giving him a star, the star has acted as a positive reinforcer for the pupil's work; and when a teacher increases a pupil's work rate by removing an object from his desk with which he was playing, the object has acted as a negative reinforcer for the pupil's work.

As well as emphasizing that a reinforcer can only be defined by its consequences, that is, it maintains or increases the rate of a prior behaviour, it must also be emphasized that a reinforcer may be specific to one kind of behaviour.

Consider a pupil who chats a lot to his friends seated around him. When the teacher puts him in another desk away from his friends, he works more and chats less. When she puts him back with his friends, his chatting increases again, and his work rate drops.

In this example, being separated from his friends has reinforced the pupil's work behaviour, but not his chatting behaviour, and being put back has reinforced his chatting, but not his work.

This kind of analysis of behaviour is fundamental to behaviour modification. Consequently, if a pupil's behaviour is to be changed, it is first necessary to identify what is reinforcing the behaviour. In the examples just quoted, this seems a simple task. However, what reinforces one pupil may not reinforce another. The promise of a games lesson may reinforce some pupils, but not others, and it may be recalled that the possibility of trading in points for badminton, table tennis or snooker was completely ineffective with Teddy. Even one particular pupil may not always be reinforced by the same event. A pupil learning to read may initially find teacher attention to be reinforcing, but if the session goes on long enough, the attention will very likely lose its reinforcing value.

Ways of Decreasing Behaviour

In the discussion of reinforcers, there has been a certain emphasis on ways of increasing behaviours. Naturally enough, teachers wish to see this happen with some behaviours. On the other hand, there are those pupil behaviours which the teacher would like to decrease, for example, pupils talking when they should be working, interrupting the teacher when he is talking, disturbing other pupils. These are the kinds of behaviour which, when carried to excess, may attract sanctions such as detention, lines or caning. Teachers who are skilled in behaviour modification techniques use alternative procedures.

Extinction

Behaviour will be extinguished, if whatever is reinforcing the behaviour can be identified and removed. This would be a very simple procedure to apply if reinforcers could be immediately identified, and if they could be easily removed. In practice, a teacher has to use his professional judgement in selecting what appears to be the reinforcer, and his professional skills in arranging removal of that reinforcer. He can only judge if he has been accurate in his selection of the reinforcer, and efficient in its removal, by a process of continual systematic observation.

Consider the pupil who continually demands teacher attention. He comes out to the desk asking unnecessary questions, or he sits looking helpless and puzzled when the class has just been told what to do, and when the teacher knows that he is quite capable of understanding the instructions which have been given to the class. For this pupil, teacher attention seems to be a reinforcer which is maintaining the behaviour. He gets the attention, and later, he repeats the behaviour. Removing the teacher's attention would seem to be the appropriate treatment.

For another pupil, a teacher may decide that a change of seating will remove reinforcement from an unwanted behaviour; for example, if the pupil has been talking a lot to his friends seated nearby, when he ought to have been working. The pupil may talk less, at least initially, when seated away from his friends.

It is however, comparatively rare to find a pupil behaviour which is maintained by a single reinforcer, and this being so, any treatment based on a single reinforcer may well be ineffective. It is true that a teacher's attention may be a powerful reinforcer for the behaviour of certain pupils, but very often peer-group attention can be equally if not more reinforcing. There is also the possibility that withdrawal of a reinforcer can produce other behaviours. If, for example, the teacher removes his attention from a pupil's behaviour, there is a danger that the behaviour may escalate into an even more unwanted form.

In a similar way, the pupil who is removed to another part of the classroom to stop him talking to his friends, may decide that the best means of communication lies in raising his voice, which is likely to be more disruptive than was his original behaviour.

However, whilst it is obviously difficult to decrease a behaviour in the classroom by removing reinforcement, it is much less difficult to do this when teaching a single pupil. There are fewer extraneous sources of reinforcement available, and this can be a very productive technique in such situations.

Perhaps the major weakness of this technique in the classroom, is that the teacher is using the principles of behaviour modification only to decrease unwanted behaviour. When reinforcement is removed from the unwanted behaviour, the pupil is likely to seek out other reinforcers, and perhaps to try out other behaviours in an effort to extract further reinforcement. It is at this time, that the teacher ought to be reinforcing other, more appropriate, behaviours.

Reinforcing an Incompatible Behaviour

A more realistic means of decreasing a behaviour is to reinforce an incompatible behaviour, that is, a behaviour which precludes the unwanted behaviour. If a teacher wishes to decrease the time a pupil spends out of his desk, he must reinforce the pupil when he is in his desk. If a teacher wishes to decrease the time a pupil spends talking to his friends, he must reinforce the pupil for doing his work. If a teacher wishes to stop pupils shouting out answers to his questions, he must only reinforce those pupils who put up their hands. A good example of the successful use of this procedure was seen in the case of Frank, when Mrs Jones ignored his inappropriate behaviours and paid attention to him when he was working.

For many pupils, a teacher's attention is in itself reinforcing. If this is so, then the teacher must be selective with his attention. It is all too easy to pay attention to a constantly misbehaving pupil, whilst he is being disruptive, and to attend to the other diligently working pupils when he is quiet. This does seem to be a reasonable way of allocating time, yet in the long term, this procedure can be self-defeating. The pupil should be reinforced for working and not for misbehaving.

If however, a teacher finds his attention is not reinforcing, he must consider using another, more intrusive method of reinforcement, such as drawing up a contract, as did some of the teachers in the cases described in the previous chapter. And since the ultimate aim must be to cease using such intrusive methods, he must continue to give his praise and attention to the pupil when providing reinforcement. In this way, the teacher himself may acquire reinforcing value.

It will have been noted that the treatment of most of the pupils whose cases are described in Chapter 1 was based upon reinforcing an incompatible behaviour. In some cases, this was combined with the use of an extinction procedure. Just why a particular method was selected depended upon a certain set of circumstances and upon a teacher's perception of these circumstances. One cannot generalize too much, but it seems clear that reinforcing incompatible behaviour can be a very successful method of decreasing unwanted behaviour.

Intermittent Reinforcement

One of the questions which teachers frequently ask when they are about to use behaviour modification principles to treat a pupil is, 'How often should I reinforce the behaviour?' This is not a question which always produces the same reply, since circumstances differ, but it is relatively easy to give guidelines.

Some behaviours in life are reinforced whenever they occur. Generally speaking, these are the behaviours which sustain life itself. Other behaviours tend to be reinforced intermittently. Diligently working pupils are reinforced occasionally by their teachers, pupils who put up their hands to answer a question are reinforced occasionally when they are allowed to answer the question.

This intermittent reinforcement can be very powerful. Consider the commercial success of the 'fruit machine'. These machines may be clearly labelled '76 per cent pay-off', yet this does not deter the player. Most of the players must know that they are going to lose in the long run, yet they continue to play. Such is the power of intermittent reinforcement.

Whilst intermittent reinforcement will maintain a behaviour, it is not a very efficient way of establishing behaviour, as any animal trainer knows. In the early stages of its development, a behaviour needs to be reinforced as frequently as possible. If a teacher is trying to help a pupil make the correct verbal response to the letter *a*, he must initially pronounce the letter himself for the pupil to imitate, and then reinforce every correct response. When this response has been made many times, continual reinforcement is neither necessary nor practical.

It is not too difficult to apply this reasoning to the setting up of the behaviour involved in playing a 'fruit machine'. Before playing the machine themselves, the potential addicts will presumably have seen someone else playing the machine and perhaps winning. Machines seem to be designed to maximize on this possibility, since winning is often accompanied by a cacophony of sound, carefully timed so as not to mask the sound of falling coins. This is to encourage imitative behaviour from the on-lookers.

In recent times, 'fruit machines' have become more complex in their operation. The more successful machines incorporate flashing lights, stop buttons, gamble buttons, and a variety of complex features. One is inevitably reminded of Skinner's (1968) comment that children will play for hours with material which 'will provide considerable automatic reinforcement, which feeds back significant changes in the environment, and is reasonably free of aversive properties'. 'Fruit machines' seem to have been designed with this quotation in mind!

When this discussion is related back to the original question posed, which was concerned with how often a behaviour should be reinforced, certain answers emerge. If a teacher wishes to increase the performance of a very infrequent behaviour, he must initially reinforce each occurrence, if this is possible. If the behaviour is occurring frequently, he should reinforce the behaviour frequently, although not necessarily each time it occurs. In the long term however, when the behaviour is well established, the frequency of reinforcement needs to be reduced, so that eventually the pupil may behave in the same way as the other pupils, under the same conditions of reinforcement. Because of the power of intermittent reinforcements, it is possible to achieve this, and some of the cases which have been previously discussed illustrate how this 'fading out' of reinforcement can be accomplished.

The power of intermittent reinforcement also explains why some unwanted pupil behaviours are so difficult to remove. It is not sufficient just to decrease the reinforcement these behaviours receive, since the occasional reinforcement remaining may still be enough to maintain the behaviour. This is one of the reasons why an extinction procedure which is not combined with the reinforcement of an incompatible behaviour may be unsuccessful. In addition to this, the power of intermittent reinforcement can make it difficult to identify what is reinforcing a particular behaviour. It becomes necessary to watch a pupil's behaviour very carefully over a long period of time, since it is unlikely that every instance of behaviour will be accompanied by the reinforcement for that behaviour.

Imitation, Chaining and Shaping

Having read the previous discussion, a teacher might well remark, 'Yes, I see how to reinforce a behaviour, but what do I do if he never performs the behaviour?' This is a fair comment. How can a teacher reinforce what never occurs?

This is the sort of problem which games teachers face very frequently. Suppose a teacher is trying to show a pupil how to use a tennis racquet properly. The behaviour he wishes to occur is a smooth, controlled stroke. He may use a number of methods to achieve this. He will show the pupil how the stroke should be made, giving him a model for imitation. He will require the pupil to make elements of the stroke, and will give verbal reinforcement for these. He will give reinforcement for successive approximations of the stroke. These three methods illustrate the three basic processes known to behaviour modifiers as imitation, chaining and shaping respectively.

Imitation

One way in which we learn is by observing others. The process of imitation or modelling, as it is sometimes called, is one of the fundamental ways in which children learn how to behave. It only takes a little casual observation of the behaviour of children and their parents to see this process in operation. Likewise, if one notes the way that parents exhort their children to play with certain individuals and not with others, one realizes that parents are well aware of the potential influences of imitation.

The possibility of imitation is always present, and this makes it difficult to discuss imitation in isolation from other processes. It has already been referred to in connection with initiating behaviours, and it is undoubtedly present continually in classrooms, when pupils see others behaving in various ways.

It is not always easy to decide how a pupil selects someone to imitate. Usually a person is selected who has reinforcing properties for the pupil, for example, a parent. Yet, the boy imitates the father's behaviour, and the girl, the mother's behaviour. This indicates that something more is involved in the selection of a model than its possession of reinforcing properties. There is also an element of discrimination present.

In the classroom, the teacher may well have reinforcing properties, yet the pupils may not imitate his patient, diligent, friendly behaviours. They may select a very different person to imitate, perhaps the most disruptive pupil. This is one reason why changing the behaviour of a disruptive pupil can have a beneficial effect on the rest of the class, for example, as in the case of Billy, described in Chapter 1.

On a more positive note, it seems likely that the pupils will imitate one of their number who has reinforcing properties within the group, say, a popular pupil, and if such a pupil can be induced to behave appropriately, the other pupils may follow suit.

At a much simpler level, imitation is clearly important when a pupil is learning to read. The teacher says the word, and the pupil repeats the word. The same basic process applies at a variety of educational levels, always provided the pupil has acquired the basic skills necessary for imitation.

Chaining

So far, behaviours have been discussed as though they are the basic elements of performance. Yet, if one examines most behaviours, they are seen to be sequences of simpler behaviours. Shouting out in class comprises a sequence of words, and doing a sum consists of a sequence of interrelated behaviours. Each complex behaviour may be regarded as a chain of simpler behaviours, the links in the chain being forged by the reinforcement at the end of the chain.

When a new, complex behaviour is to be learned, the various simple constituent behaviours have to be linked together. The simple behaviours usually link in an 'end on' manner, that is, one after another. This is particularly apparent in the phonic method of learning to read, when *c a t* has to be combined to read cat. Sometimes, however, the sequence is combined in a more complex manner, and this can make learning difficult, as anyone who has ever taught the swimming of the 'breast stroke' can appreciate. It would be so much simpler if the leg movement followed the arm movement.

Because chaining involves putting behaviours in sequence, it does seem natural that one ought to help the learner construct the chains in a forward manner, starting at the beginning. However, in certain circumstances, chaining might well be more effective if done in a 'backward' manner. Teaching a retarded pupil how to do a jigsaw puzzle might best be done by initially requiring him to put in just the final piece, and then progressively removing more pieces. In this way, the pupil can see the final product, and be more meaningfully reinforced.

Shaping

Shaping is essentially moulding behaviour into a particular form. Consider, for example, a teacher who is trying to help a child make the correct sound to the letter *b*. The teacher will say the sound, and then listen to the pupil's imitation. When the pupil makes the correct sound, reinforcement is given. For many pupils this poses little difficulty, but with the speech-deficient pupil, the teacher's objective can be very difficult to achieve. With such a pupil, the teacher must selectively reinforce successive approximations to the correct sound. Initially, it may be that the pupil is reluctant even to make an attempt, so that reinforcement must be given for any sound. Later, the form of the sound may be shaped by the selective reinforcement of small incremental steps.

When using shaping, the teacher has to make two key decisions.

He has to decide what the final behaviour is to be, and he has to decide how closely the pupil's present behaviour resembles the final behaviour. To move the pupil's present behaviour to the final behaviour may mean taking the pupil through a large number of intermediate steps.

Shaping is very much a feature of our everyday lives. We shape our children to observe correct table manners. We shape our partners to behave in certain ways. That we are not always as successful as we would like to be probably means that we ought to reconsider our procedures, and take into account the influence of other shapers and models for imitation.

Shaping does not always require that reinforcement is given by another person. Games players, for example, often improve their technique merely by playing games. This can be explained, at least in part, by the feedback they gain when they vary their behaviour. The novice tennis player who suddenly, and seemingly accidentally, produces a devastating shot will savour the moment, and seek to reproduce the behaviour. Such moments are cherished.

To return to the initial question which was posed. There are three basic processes which can be used by the teacher to set up a new behaviour. Whilst the three processes have been treated independently in the text, in practice they are often used in combination with each other. Teaching a new behaviour frequently requires that imitation, chaining and shaping are all used.

When a teacher decides to set up a new behaviour, he may find it helpful to seek the answers to the following questions:

1 What precisely is the new behaviour?
2 What is the present behaviour?
3 Is there an available, appropriate model for imitation?
4 What could be a reinforcer for the behaviour?
5 Can the behaviour be achieved by helping the pupil chain together existing behaviours?
6 What sort of approximations to the behaviour ought to be reinforced at various stages of competence?

The answers to these, and other questions which these give rise to, should aid the teacher in designing an appropriate learning programme.

Generalization and Discrimination

The term generalization was used in the previous chapter, when it was noted that whilst Arthur would talk quite freely with his teacher when alone, he would not talk so freely when they were both in the classroom. Arthur's behaviour did not generalize across the two situations. This is one aspect of generalization.

Broadly speaking, generalization can occur in three different ways, firstly across situations, secondly to behaviours other than those being treated, and thirdly to other reinforcers. In Arthur's case, the teacher was trying to achieve generalization across situations.

Generalization may occur naturally, but ideally it ought to be planned for in a programme. Such planning is evident in a number of the cases detailed in Chapter 1, when the teachers faded out the 'artificial' reinforcement, that is the pupils' behaviours were generalizing to normal classroom reinforcers. It should be remembered, however, that there was a tendency for this to occur without a conscious effort.

Whilst generalization is very important in its own right, it must be considered in conjunction with discrimination. It is difficult to think of a behaviour which should be performed in all situations. It is appropriate for a pupil to sit quietly at his desk in some lessons, but not in others. Talking loudly may not be appropriate in many lessons, but it can be in some. Pupils must learn to discriminate.

In everyday life, the ability to discriminate can be very important. The failure to discriminate from subtle cues can make a person socially inept. Teachers learn to pick up cues from their pupils' behaviour, and they themselves behave accordingly. How and when to reinforce a pupil's behaviour depends upon a teacher's discriminatory ability.

Naturally enough, pupils will learn to discriminate. They will learn what to do in one situation, and what not to do in another. Problems arise in schools when the behaviours which pupils learn to perform in the classrooms are not the behaviours which the teachers wish to see performed. One of the ways in which teachers attempt to deal with such problems is by introducing school rules. These are to enable the pupil to discriminate which behaviours are appropriate in school and in the classroom, and which are not appropriate. Since the classroom rules must differ necessarily from one lesson to another, for example, from Mathematics to Drama, the pupil must learn to discriminate, and not generalize his behaviour from one lesson to another. If, however, the 'rules' differ from one teacher to another, as may sometimes occur, this poses some difficulties in discrimination. This is, of course, exacerbated in large secondary schools in which pupils may be taught by as many as eight different teachers in a day. If, in addition to this, any one teacher is inconsistent in his application of the rules, the pupil must find it very difficult to discriminate just what he may or may not do.

It may be that the problems which can arise from an inappropriate use of school rules have been exaggerated, and that pupils are more capable of discriminating than has been suggested. On the other hand, it is worth examining a pupil's understanding of the rules before embarking on a programme which seeks to change behaviours encompassed by the rules.

Another, related problem which concerns teachers is the behaviour which they feel has generalized from the pupils' homes. When a pupil's behaviour in school is inappropriate to his surroundings, it is tempting to conclude that this is how he has learned to behave at home. This conclusion may well be correct. However, as Rutter *et al.* (1979) point out, 'For almost a dozen years during a formative period of their development children spend almost as much of their waking life at school as at home. Altogether this works out at some 15,000 hours.' This does give the schools considerable time in which to help pupils to learn appropriate behaviours.

It may well be, however, that what occurs during the first five years of a child's life has a very strong effect on his future behaviour, and it may also be true that the home, and later the peer group, possesses more powerful reinforcers for the pupil than does the school. However, whilst the pupil may generalize behaviours from one situation to another, he is also capable of discrimination. If the pupil is to learn, he must be helped to discriminate between acceptable and unacceptable behaviour in school. This does not imply that his home background should be ignored. In fact, the more a teacher knows about a pupil's home, the better will he be able to help the pupil. The teacher will be better able to discriminate how to reinforce the pupil's appropriate behaviour. If, in addition, the aid of parents can be enlisted, as happens in a number of schools, the school and home can operate as mutually reinforcing systems for the pupil's various appropriate behaviours, both inside and outside school.

This may seem to be an overly optimistic appraisal of what can be done. Yet it is no more than sensitive teachers have been doing for many years, with considerable success.

Some Other Practices

The earlier parts of this chapter have outlined the more theoretical aspects of behaviour modification, and should serve to explain why certain procedures were adopted in the treatment of the pupils described in Chapter 1. However, it will probably have been noticed that not all the procedures used, for example, contracting and self-recording, have as yet been discussed. In addition, to make the coverage of behaviour modification practices more complete, two other procedures, the use of tokens and time-out, need to be discussed.

Contracting

Entering into a contract with a pupil may seem a strange procedure to adopt in a classroom. Yet contracts are very much a feature of our society. We enter into contracts when we buy houses, when we marry, and when we enter into employment. Contracts of one kind or another are inescapable. Indeed, in recent years there has been an increasing emphasis on specifying the exact nature of a contract, as all teachers will appreciate. In this sense, it could be argued that entering into a contract could be very beneficial to a pupil. It could be an aid to him in his future handling of contractual obligations.

A moment of reflection on our school system indicates that there are a number of what might be called 'negative contracts' in operation. They are not always explicitly stated, nor are they always formalized, but they do exist. Consider the following statements:

'If you carry on fooling about, you will have to complete your work during break-time.'

'If this behaviour occurs again, we shall have to suspend you from school.'

If these are not contracts, they are idle threats, and as such seem doomed to disaster.

There are of course some 'positive contracts' in operation in schools. Pupils generally know under what conditions they can receive a prize or a commendation at school assembly. However, these positive contracts do tend to be less frequently expressed than negative contracts.

Perhaps the most unfortunate aspect of positive contracts is that they tend to be fulfilled by the best pupils. We ought perhaps to turn our attention to those pupils who receive little from such contracts. Teachers may well agree with this sentiment, but may still feel worried that entering into a contract with one pupil will have a deleterious effect on the other pupils in the class. This is a very reasonable cause for concern. Yet it may be an unjustified fear. In the case of Tom, described in Chapter 1, a relatively comprehensive contract was devised and fulfilled. However, because Tom's teacher was concerned about the effect this might have on the whole class, the behaviour of other pupils was observed throughout the whole period of the investigation. The results clearly indicated that, rather than deteriorating, the behaviour of the other pupils actually improved.

Whilst for the sake of clarity, the full details of this case were not presented in Chapter 1, they may be found by consulting Harrop (1978a).

It cannot be concluded from this one investigation that making a contract with one pupil will never have a deleterious effect on other pupils. On the other hand, it can certainly be concluded that making a contract can, in certain circumstances, be beneficial both to the pupil concerned and to the class.

If a teacher decides to enter into a contract with a pupil, he may find the following guidelines to be helpful. The book *How to Use Contingency Contracting in the Classroom*, written by Lloyd Homme in 1969, offers a number of suggestions, which are listed below in an abbreviated form:

1 The pay-off should be immediate, especially in the early stages.
2 It is better to provide frequent, small rewards for slight improvements in behaviour, rather than large rewards for a great change in behaviour.
3 Both sides of the agreement should appear balanced to the participants; that is, a pupil should not be contracted to receive a reward either for too little, or for too much work.
4 Because of the different levels of pupils' ability, it is better to arrange individual rather than group contracts.
5 The tasks involved in the contract must be able to be completed in the available time.

When to use a contract is a decision that the teacher is best able to take, and to a large extent this decision depends upon the severity of the pupil's difficulties. However, using a contract when less artificial methods may work, is a little like using a sledgehammer to crack a nut.

Self-Recording

Self-recording requires a pupil to observe his own behaviour in a systematic manner, as was seen in the case of Joe, described in the previous chapter. It is not a procedure which has been very widely used in schools, but it is quite common in other spheres of activity. Many individuals have found that recording some aspect of their behaviour has enabled them to modify that behaviour. This is particularly evident when people wish to control their weight.

The results of self-recording procedures in schools have not always been successful, as McNamara (1978) has noted. A potential weakness of the technique is that records can be falsified. For this reason it is important to have an independent check made on recordings. This independent check need not be continuous, but it is important that the pupil should not know when it is to be made. If the pupil does know when the check is made, there is a risk that self-recorded data will be accurate only when it is being checked.

Provided self-recording is done accurately, there are two advantages to be gained by using this technique. First, it can yield data from a variety of lessons taken by several teachers, and secondly, it shifts some of the responsibility on to the pupil – that is, it is a step towards the development of self-control. These two advantages indicate why self-recording is perhaps more appropriately used in the secondary school than in the primary school. At the secondary stage of education, the pupil is likely to be taught by several teachers in the course of one day, and he is fast reaching an age at which self-control is very important.

The Use of Tokens

When we think of tokens, we tend to picture individuals receiving points, stars, or even pieces of plastic, which can later be exchanged for something more desirable. This may seem to be a very artificial way of interacting with pupils, yet, on reflection, our everyday existence is seen to involve the use of tokens. What is money if it isn't a token? There is not a lot we can do with it, except exchange it for something more desirable.

All schools use tokens. House-points, stars, and even marks on books are tokens of one kind or another. However, when a behaviour modifier uses tokens, he is usually going beyond this normal usage.

The token used can be anything from a mark on a book to a plastic star, just so long as it is not something which can be manufactured by a pupil without the teacher's knowledge. Provided the token is firmly associated by the pupil with something that he wants, the token can be a very effective reinforcer.

Tokens are used because they have several advantages over other kinds of reinforcement. Some of these advantages are listed below:

1 Pupils often need very frequent signs that they are behaving appropriately. Tokens can supply these signs.

2 Tokens need not be tied to a single reinforcer like teacher's praise, which may lose its effectiveness from time to time. They can be cashed for a variety of reinforcers.
3 Tokens can be applied for a variety of behaviours.
4 Tokens offer the possibility of obtaining a larger reinforcer than would normally be the case when a single reinforcer is used, since tokens may be saved over a period of time.

Token systems can be very effective. However, it is no coincidence that token systems tend to flourish in special schools rather than in ordinary schools. There seems really very little need for an ordinary school to become involved in an overly elaborate token system. However, equally, there seems no logical reason why the use of tokens should be completely ignored when house-points and stars are used in general practice.

Consider the following case, in which a teacher, in consultation with the writer, treated a pupil in a remedial class who was very reluctant to stay at his desk. The teacher talked with the pupil, who was nine years old, and explained to him as carefully as possible the desirability of staying at his desk and working. He was quite sympathetic to her view, but was clearly unimpressed by the long term advantages of working. When the teacher asked him what he would prefer to be doing, she received a list of suggestions. From amongst this list, she extracted as a potential reinforcer the fact that he claimed to want her attention for his reading.

Armed with this information, the teacher made a contract with the pupil that whenever he worked in his desk for half an hour, this would be followed by a spell of such reading. The pupil agreed that this was a very satisfactory arrangement. However, he did not fulfil his part of the contract. He did not stay in his desk.

The teacher was left in something of a dilemma. The pupil still expressed the desire to read to her, yet he seemingly couldn't manage half an hour at his desk. She was reluctant to reduce the time period, since this would disrupt her work with the other pupils, yet a reduced time period did seem to be required.

As a way out of the dilemma, the teacher decided to use a token procedure. She told the pupil that she would initial his book every five minutes during which he stayed in his desk working. When he had collected six such initials, not necessarily consecutively, he could read to her. This worked well. At first, the five minute periods occurred spasmodically throughout the lesson, but gradually, they became consecutive.

In this case, it seemed quite evident that the use of tokens was beneficial to the pupil. The signatures had acted as signs that he had fulfilled at least part of his contract. He was able to save these signatures until he had sufficient 'currency' to obtain his reward.

This case also reveals another interesting feature of behaviour modification. The teacher selected a pay-off reinforcer which was educationally beneficial to the pupil. This should not go unnoticed at this stage, and it is a consideration which will be returned to later.

Time-Out

This is a procedure which is used to reduce inappropriate behaviour by removing a pupil from access to reinforcement. At its most extreme, it can mean isolating a pupil for a time in a bare room devoid of any feature which might interest him. This is essentially an extension of the extinction procedure, which seeks to remove reinforcement from inappropriate behaviours. However, unlike the extinction procedure, time-out involves a physical movement of the pupil away from other available reinforcers.

Such a procedure might, at best, make teachers feel uneasy. Yet, what of the boy or girl in a school for maladjusted pupils, who is sometimes physically aggressive, and is a danger to other pupils? A few brief periods of time-out may stop this behaviour. Moreover, if time-out is not used, the alternative treatment may involve the permanent removal of the pupil from his peer group. Under circumstances like this, the use of time-out merits consideration.

Time-out can be a very successful procedure, and its success can be achieved with very few removals. However, it is all too easy for the teacher unwittingly to help the treatment fail by his very concern for the pupil he is treating. He can make the time-out room a comfortable, interesting area, and pop in and out to see how the pupil is faring, with the result that the pupil may find time-out to be reinforcing. Obviously, the pupil needs to be watched during time-out, but this must be done unobtrusively, otherwise he may find the attention reinforcing.

At a less extreme level, a time-out procedure can be used without a special room being involved. For some pupils, the use of a time-out area in a classroom can be effective, provided other sources of reinforcement for inappropriate behaviour are not available. This may, however, be difficult to achieve.

In general, the use of time-out procedures is not really appropriate with pupils in ordinary schools, since pupils whose behaviours are of sufficient magnitude to suggest the procedure ought not be found in such schools.

Summary

Throughout this chapter there has been a continual emphasis on the consequences of behaviour, and of the reinforcing properties of these consequences. It has been seen that under various circumstances, a pupil can be reinforced by the material he is learning, by a teacher's attention, by a token, and by a whole variety of events. It has been stressed that reinforcement must be used selectively in order to help a pupil overcome his classroom difficulties.

Procedures for increasing and decreasing rates of behaviour have been discussed, and these various procedures have been seen to differ in the degree of artificiality they introduce into the classroom. The relative usefulness of continuous and intermittent reinforcement has been emphasized, with some indication of when each is best used; whilst at the same time the danger of maintaining an unwanted behaviour by intermittent reinforcement has been indicated.

In addition to examining consequences, the associated processes of generalization and discrimination have been outlined, together with the implications these have for the teacher. Finally, the process of imitation has been discussed, in conjunction with chaining and shaping, two processes which are concerned with consequences of behaviour.

Taken as a whole, this chapter may be said to have addressed itself to answering two general questions:

1. Why is a pupil behaving in a particular way in the classroom?
2. What can the teacher do if he wishes to modify the pupil's behaviour?

Chapter 3

Translating the Principles and Procedures into Practice

Any experienced teacher reading this book will almost certainly have noticed that many of the elements of behaviour modification exist in the current practices of teaching. Within the classroom, the teacher strives to make work interesting yet academically appropriate to the pupils' needs. He pays attention to his pupils and shows appreciation of good work. He verbally checks behaviour which infringes the rules. For many teachers, and many pupils, this is all that is needed. Would that it were always so.

One way in which current practice departs from the procedures generally used by behaviour modifiers lies in the use of disapproval. White (1975), in a survey which involved classroom observations of 104 teachers in the USA, found that verbal disapproval exceeded verbal approval at all grade levels beyond a pupil age of six, roughly equivalent to the infant school level. Moreover, this difference became disproportionately larger as the pupil was older. Thomas *et al.* (1978) conducted a similar survey in New Zealand, with teachers of pupils aged eleven to thirteen, and obtained very similar results, that is, for this age range, the ratio of disapproval to approval was approximately 3:1.

It is quite true that since these investigations were carried out in the USA, and New Zealand, they do not necessarily apply in Britain. However, consider the work of Rutter *et al.* (1979), in which twelve secondary schools in London were surveyed to see what impact the schools had on their pupils. This was research on a very large scale, over two thousand pupils being followed through their secondary schools. Data was collected on the pupils' attendance, examination results, behaviour in school and delinquency out of school. Whilst the findings of this investigation were necessarily complex and detailed, significantly, amongst the findings, it was noted that across the whole sample of schools the classroom observations showed that teachers' reprimands occurred twice as frequently as teacher's praise.

This predominance of reprimands may be no surprise. What may surprise teachers was the further finding that teachers' praise was associated with better pupil behaviour and lower delinquency rates, whilst teachers' reprimands showed no such relationships. When other school practices were examined, it was found that 'Whilst the links between punishment and outcome were rather variable, those between rewards and outcome were more consistent. All forms of rewards, praise or appreciation tended to be associated with better outcomes.'

Rewards and Punishments within the Schools

If one examines practices within schools, a number of potential rewards and punishments may be distinguished. Apart from teachers' praise and admonitions, these include the use of stars, house-points, prizes, detention, lines and caning. The relative use of these varies from school to school, and indeed from one classroom to another within the same school. Additionally, it is difficult to separate these practices from the teachers who apply them, since it is quite evident in schools that pupils do not respond in exactly the same way to the same practices when applied by different teachers.

There are of course different personal philosophies surrounding the use of these practices. Some teachers dislike stars because they feel that pupils become involved in competition, and that less able pupils lose out. Some teachers give stars for effort, whilst others feel this practice is difficult to justify to more able pupils. Other teachers may use class-stars, so that a class competes against its own score of the previous week.

Similar comments may be made about the use of house-points. In addition, house-points may suffer from 'galloping inflation'. If one teacher distributes house-points more liberally than his colleagues, they may feel that their currency has been devalued. The pay-off for house-points is another important feature of their use. If the gaining of house-points results in embarrassment for some of the pupils at the end of the week, then such a system can be counter-productive. If, on the other hand, competition is seen to be fair, that is, all houses have an equal chance of doing well, and the pay-off rewards the pupils in a meaningful way, then the use of house-points can be very effective. In practice, it is rather difficult to arrange that these conditions are met. All too often, one house seems to contain a preponderance of pupils who gain house-points, whilst another seems to lack such pupils. Also, it is not always easy to arrange a reward which is appreciated by pupils of different ages. A word of praise from the headmaster may be an effective reward for the younger children in a secondary school, but it may well embarrass older pupils.

The giving of prizes for performance seems to be fraught with less difficulty. However, prizes do seem to go to the more academic, or to the more athletic. The competition may be fair in the sense that prizes are open to all, yet some pupils have in-built advantages. If prizes were to be awarded on the basis of effort, then competition would really be fair. However, a moment's consideration shows this to be an impossible task. How can an accurate measure of effort be made? Certainly progress prizes are sometimes awarded, but it is rather difficult to assess to whom these ought to be given.

When one looks at detention, lines and caning, these are seen to be much simpler to apply. They are usually given when a pupil infringes the rules of the school, and as such, they are aimed at discouraging 'bad' behaviour and by implication at encouraging 'good' behaviour.

In practice, detention means keeping a pupil in a classroom, usually doing school work when he would normally be free. Giving a pupil lines, means that the pupil writes out something during his free time. Caning means that the pupil is struck with a cane by the teacher. These practices may discourage a pupil from repeating the behaviour which precipitated such treatment. However, when such practices are repeatedly administered, the pupil is likely to learn to associate the school and the teachers with unpleasant consequences. These practices may improve the behaviour of certain pupils, although the work of Rutter *et al.* (1979) suggests that this is not so in general (indeed quite the reverse for corporal punishment), even so, it is difficult to see how they can encourage a pupil to find the school to be a rewarding environment.

There are many other practices of a less formal nature carried out in schools. Sending a disruptive pupil to stand outside the door of the classroom is a well-worn procedure. Very often this acts as a reward to the pupil. He enjoys the recognition this bestows upon him, and he may even make grimaces through the window when the teacher isn't looking. Such actions are generally well rewarded by his peers.

Sometimes pupils are sent to the headteacher as a punishment for breaking rules. Pupils are sent less frequently as a reward. This differential must have an effect on the way pupils view the headteacher. From time to time, a teacher may send pupil after pupil to the headteacher because of misbehaviour. This can become a dilemma for the headteacher, who begins to wonder if it is always the pupils who are at fault. If strong measures are taken, is this fair to the pupils? If strong measures are not taken, is this fair to the teacher?

The overall picture of schools that this discussion produces is one in which there is a balance between rewards and punishments. Rewards are less easy to apply than are punishments, yet rewards do seem to be associated with appropriate pupil behaviours, whilst punishments do not. That schools must have sanctions is evident, but they must not be over-used. How to increase the effectiveness of both punishments and rewards is a central issue in education.

Effective Punishment

The one aspect of behaviour modification techniques which teachers find most difficult to accept is the playing down of the use of punishment. The practice of removing reinforcers from 'unwanted' behaviours and reinforcing incompatible behaviours is usually followed with the pupil who misbehaves. However, as was mentioned earlier, it is not always possible in a classroom to remove all the reinforcers which maintain a behaviour. Consequently, an unwanted behaviour may continue unabated, or it may begin to escalate. In addition, the teacher may see signs in the classroom that unwanted behaviour is becoming contagious. When such circumstances occur, some form of punishment is necessary. If punishment is to be used, it must be used effectively and sparingly.

The nature of the punishment adminstered must be such that it does suppress the unwanted behaviour. To an extent, the kind of punishment which is effective varies from one pupil to another, so that a sharp word from a teacher may be very strong punishment for one pupil, and completely ineffective for another. Because of this it is very difficult to generalize, although a recent survey of 875 secondary school pupils, aged eleven to fifteen years, conducted by Burns (1978), found that boys listed corporal punishment, an unfavourable report sent home, and detention as the three most disliked deterrents, whilst girls listed corporal punishment, an unfavourable report sent home, and being made to look foolish in class by means of sarcasm, as their three. The least disliked deterrents were, for boys, being urged to make an effort, being made to look foolish in class jokingly, and a good talking to in private; and for girls, being sent from the room, a good talking to in private, and being urged to make an effort. These lists are however merely indicators, since deterrents which are disliked are not necessarily deterrents which are effective.

If punishment is to be associated with an infringement of rules, the time gap between the infringement and the punishment ought to be as brief as possible. The longer the delay, the weaker will be the association. Sometimes a system of 'minus points' is used, and provided the pupil understands why he receives such a point, this can bridge the time gap between the infringement and the punishment. In addition, if as commonly occurs, a certain number of these points have to be collected before a punishment is administered, the pupil may learn to exert control over his behaviour, although clearly this procedure raises problems of how many points to administer for a particular infringement, and of how many points are added together to justify the final punishment.

Whilst punishment may be necessary from time to time, it is not difficult to see the dangers inherent in its use. If a pupil is not clear why he receives punishment, he may reduce his general level of behaviour in school, he may feel unjustly treated, and he may feel that he cannot establish satisfactory relationships with teachers. If punishment is too severe, it may lead the pupil to avoid teachers, and to avoid school. If punishment is too frequent, the pupil may learn to associate the teachers and the school with unpleasant consequences.

It is very difficult to summarize how punishment may best be used. However, when it has to be used, it seems evident that:

1. It ought to be used to help a pupil discriminate rules which are not to be broken.
2. The teacher must be completely consistent in his punishment for rule breaking.
3. The punishment must be aversive to the pupil, although not too severe.
4. The punishment ought to be administered as soon after the infringement as possible.

When these four conditions are observed, as indeed they are by many teachers, punishment does not have to be administered frequently.

Effective Rewards

It would seem logical to follow a section on effective punishment with a discussion of effective rewards. However, since the effective use of rewards is a theme which runs throughout the text, and has not yet been developed fully, such a section would necessarily be incomplete at this stage.

The Role of the Teacher in Behaviour Modification

It is in the application of behaviour modification techniques to the classroom that one sees most clearly an examination of the effectiveness of the use of rewards. This was illustrated in the eight cases discussed in Chapter 1. Moreover, it may seem that the role of the teacher in using rewards, and in behaviour modification in general, has already been clearly explained. This is not really so. What was really seen in Chapter 1 was 'the tip of the iceberg', to use a popular but curiously appropriate analogy.

Beneath the obvious features of what the teachers actually did, and the apparent simplicity of phrases like 'the teacher was concerned that', and 'the teacher decided to', there lurks a huge mass of complex considerations and decisions which had to be taken.

These considerations begin inevitably with the realization that no two pupils are alike. Each is a unique individual with a different genetic endowment and a different environmental background. Even identical twins cannot have exactly the same environment.

When this is examined at the level of the classroom, large differences along many dimensions are seen between pupils. Equally, large differences may exist between classes of pupils, and between the teachers of these classes. Because of all these differences, it is not possible to lay down courses of action to be followed without very careful consideration.

The person who is uniquely qualified to understand the complexities involved is the teacher. Who else can appreciate the difficulties a pupil experiences in the classroom? Who else can appreciate what might reinforce the pupil when he is amongst his peers? Because only he can answer such questions, the teacher has to be the decision maker as well as the practitioner. Behaviour modification can inform him of available procedures, of theoretical considerations, and of what has worked for other teachers with other pupils, but it cannot tell the teacher what will work with his pupils in his classroom.

Let us look briefly at some of the decisions a teacher must make when he wishes to use behaviour modification techniques to help a pupil overcome difficulties. These decisions have already been referred to in the cases discussed in Chapter 1, but not in the systematic form which follows.

1 The teacher must first seek to analyze the precise nature of the pupil's difficulties, and must satisfy himself that the answer is

not to be found in a more appropriate use of curriculum material.

2 If no answer is to be found in the curriculum material, the teacher must specify the difficulties in behavioural terms.
3 The teacher must decide how best to obtain a baseline estimate of the behaviours of concern. This involves a number of interrelated decisions. The behaviours may be very frequent, and therefore it may be necessary to take a time sample. The behaviours may occur at specific times during particular lessons, so that observations need to be made at these times. The original list drawn up for observation may include too many behaviours for accurate observation, so that it may have to be pruned to contain only those behaviours most central to the pupil's difficulties.
4 The teacher must decide how he can unobtrusively observe the pupil's behaviour.
5 The teacher must decide how long to continue the baseline observations in order to gain an accurate estimate of the extent of the pupil's difficulties.
6 Armed with the baseline data, the teacher must decide what to do in order to bring about an improvement in the pupil's behaviour. This is, of course, by far the most important and sensitive decision which has to be made. The teacher will know basically what changes in behaviour he would like to produce, but he must make precise decisions on how these changes may be brought about.

   When deciding what strategy to use, the teacher has to make very careful decisions about the potential reinforcers available in the classroom, how these affect the pupil, how special treatment of one pupil might affect other pupils, and whether to introduce more artificial procedures into the classroom. Yet, at the same time, he has to balance these decisions against the ultimate goal of withdrawing special treatment from the pupil. Withdrawal of treatment has to be allowed for at this stage of planning.
7 When a strategy is put into action, the teacher must continually evaluate its success, or otherwise. If the results are not those he seeks to achieve, fresh decisions have to be made.
8 Should the treatment be successful, the teacher must judge at which point he begins to fade out the treatment. Any complications at this stage must necessarily produce a new set of decisions to be made.

All these and many other related decisions have to be made by the teacher who applies behaviour modification procedures. Yet, despite the seemingly exhaustive list of decisions to be made, there are numerous important considerations which may spring to mind, that have not yet been mentioned. For example, a teacher may decide to give more attention to a pupil when he is working; but how is this to be done? What does the teacher say, or do? How often does he approach the pupil? Might too frequent attention be counter-productive? These are all pertinent questions which have to be answered by the teacher. Just what kind of answers emerge depends to a large extent upon the teacher's professional skills and his knowledge of the pupil.

Whilst this analysis of the decisions made by a teacher serves as a good illustration of the teacher's role in behaviour modification, it will probably have been noted that it did make two assumptions, (a) that the teacher was with the same class all the time, and (b) that the teacher was concerned primarily with social aspects of his pupil's difficulties. This limits the explanatory value of the discussion, and precipitates further consideration of the teacher's role.

The Secondary School

In the secondary school a teacher may take a class as infrequently as once a week, or perhaps at most six times a week for a forty minute lesson. This contrasts very markedly with the situation in the primary school, in which a teacher remains with a class for much of the day. Whilst the primary school teacher constantly interacts with some thirty pupils, the secondary school teacher will interact with a much larger number of pupils. If, for example, he teaches eight different classes, he may interact with some 240 pupils in a week.

A similar situation exists when one examines the pupil's position. In the secondary school, he may be taught by up to eight different teachers in a day, and perhaps by some fifteen different teachers in a week.

It is true that the secondary school teacher may well teach a pupil for more than one year, whereas this is unusual in the primary school. However, the time a secondary school teacher spends with any one pupil is unlikely to approach the time spent by a primary school teacher with his pupils. In addition, the relative sizes of the schools tends to exacerbate this differential. Primary schools are generally much smaller than secondary schools, and it is relatively easy in the primary school for the teacher to maintain a relationship with a pupil who has moved on to another teacher. It is also relatively easy for the primary teacher to gain information about a pupil from other teachers. There are fewer teachers to consult. The secondary teacher is involved in a much more complex network of interactions. Not only does he interact with many more pupils, he also interacts with many more staff. It is difficult under these circumstances for him to get to know all his pupils well.

Teachers in secondary schools are very aware of this difficulty, and various organizational procedures have been developed, aimed at ensuring that the individual pupil is not overlooked within the system. These procedures take various forms, and include the provision of form teachers, tutor groups, pastoral care teachers, and year headteachers. The teachers filling these posts are concerned with all aspects of the progress of certain pupils within the school.

Despite the substantial differences between secondary and primary schools, it is still quite possible for a secondary school teacher to treat a pupil whilst teaching a class. This can yield considerable success, although clearly it depends on the number of lessons per week in which treatment can be applied. Such treatment does assume that pupils can discriminate how to behave towards different teachers, yet this is not an unrealistic assumption when one looks at the way pupils generally behave with different teachers. Indeed, it could well be argued that teachers have always used behaviour modification techniques informally, with varying degrees of success with different pupils.

If, alternatively, it is decided that a pupil's difficulties are sufficiently general that he ought to be treated across a series of lessons, this is a decision which needs to be made by a group of teachers. Such a suggestion is most likely to come from a teacher responsible for pastoral care, perhaps after the pupil's difficulties have been continually brought to his attention. Under these circumstances, it might be decided that the pupil ought to be treated by all or some of his teachers. This would require a good deal of close collaboration. All the decisions outlined earlier, for example, the curriculum material, the precise nature of the difficulties, the behaviours to be observed, would be much more difficult to take.

There are however, certain advantages to be obtained from such a group approach. When baseline recordings are taken, a clear indication of the pupil's behaviour in specific lessons may be seen. An analysis of the reasons for this behaviour may give good indications for subsequent treatment. Likewise, when a strategy is implemented, any varying levels of success obtained by different teachers can yield useful information for further decisions. Equally advantageous is the fact that a group of teachers is continually involved in a dialogue aimed primarily at alleviating the difficulties which a pupil is experiencing in school.

One obvious disadvantage of this group approach lies in its complexity and the amount of discussion time it necessitates. It requires a good deal of planning, discussion and openness between teachers. Because of this, the procedure could not be used to treat a number of pupils at any one time, otherwise the teachers would spend all their time in discussion. Yet it must be added that elements of this process have always been present in schools. Teachers who are concerned about pupils do have discussions with their colleagues, they do discuss how the pupils might best be treated, and they are always willing to seek and give advice.

As a labour-saving procedure, the use of pupil self-recording has much to offer the secondary school teacher. Using this procedure, the teacher responsible for pastoral care can reduce the demands on his colleagues. After discussion, he can take most of the decisions himself, and free the teachers concerned from the necessity of group meetings, and from much of the observing, although they do need to make occasional, unobtrusive checks on the pupil's recording.

Since the very act of self-recording is frequently sufficient to alter a pupil's behaviour, it may be that no other strategy needs to be devised, other than a discussion between the teacher responsible for pastoral care and the pupil concerned, with the consequent setting up of categories of behaviour to be recorded. Should a specific treatment be necessary, this can be devised in consultation with the teachers who are concerned, and the pupil can be the observer.

This procedure is an extremely useful way of obtaining information about a pupil's behaviour across a whole sequence of lessons, and provided that the occasional, unobtrusive observations taken by teachers show that the pupil is recording accurately, a good deal of information can be obtained on the pupil's progress. And it must be re-emphasized that the pupil is not being used merely as a recording instrument. That he should learn to observe his own behaviour is an integral part of the treatment.

The Primary and Secondary School

Whilst it was felt to be necessary to devote a section to the complexities inherent in the organization of the secondary school, and the implications this may have for the application of behaviour modification techniques, there is little in the section which is not relevant to the primary school. There is no reason why several teachers who take the same class should not combine to treat a pupil, and equally, there is no reason why an able pupil should not self-record. In addition, the use of the contracts and tokens are applicable in both primary and secondary schools.

Modifying the Behaviour of more than one Pupil

When a teacher uses a behaviour modification procedure to treat one pupil, he generally does this in the presence of other pupils in the class. Should he be successful in his treatment of the pupil, it is quite likely that he will incorporate something of this treatment in his handling of other pupils, perhaps the emphasis on classroom rules, or the selective use of reinforcement. In an informal sense, he will then be treating the whole class.

The main difficulty in treating a whole class lies in the potential complexity of teacher behaviour that could be demanded by an ambitious programme. To try to treat different pupils in different ways in an attempt to modify different kinds of behaviour, might put an impossible burden on the teacher's capacity. Now it is recognized that teachers do this continually in an informal way, but to use a behaviour modification procedure effectively, the teacher would need to be very consistent, and to record accurately, and clearly this imposes very real limits on one individual.

There is no reason, of course, why a teacher should not treat a whole class of pupils if he feels that there are certain common behaviours which are interfering with learning in the classroom. At a very simple level, he may decide to treat 'shouting out' when pupils ought to be raising their hands quietly, or 'moving around' when pupils ought to be at their desks working. The treatment of a class which has these kinds of inappropriate behaviours is very similar to the treatment of one pupil. Essentially the same decisions have to be made.

Academic Performance

Not very much has been said so far about academic performance. There has been a necessary emphasis on examining the curriculum to ensure it is appropriate for the pupil, and on the use of imitation, chaining and shaping in the acquisition of skills, but little else has been discussed. This is largely because the kinds of pupil difficulty that teachers raise with behaviour modifiers tend to be of a social nature. However, this does not mean that behaviour modification procedures cannot be applied to academic behaviours.

In Chapter 1, the treatment of 'Teddy' was seen to be focussed on work done during English lessons, and it was shown that Teddy's academic output increased when a suitable reinforcer was identified and applied. Likewise, the contract made with 'Tom' included a precisely stated number of sums or problems to be completed during number lessons, and a set amount of work to be produced during language lessons.

This concentration on academic performance has considerable value. Increasing a pupil's academic performance is one of the fundamental aims of a school, and diligent work from a pupil is a behaviour which is incompatible with many other unwanted behaviours.

It is in the measurement of academic performance that problems arise. Over a very short time-period, it may be seen that a pupil's measured output of academic work can be increased, but in the longer term, difficulties emerge. If a pupil is progressing academically, he must necessarily move on continually to different, more appropriate curriculum material. When the material changes, it becomes difficult to compare the pupil's output with his previous level of performance. This makes an accurate measurement of output difficult to achieve. On the other hand, there is no reason why other indices of measurement may not be employed. For example, it is sometimes difficult to 'persuade' a pupil to hand in his homework regularly. A baseline measure could be taken of homework handed in. A potential reinforcer could be identified and applied, or a contract could be made, and the effects of this on future homework could be evaluated.

In the very long term, perhaps over the course of a year, standardised tests might be used. The pupil's initial performance on such a test could act as a baseline. A strategy could be implemented through the year, and the treatment could be evaluated by the pupil's performance on an alternative form of the test at the end of the year, although care would need to be taken to ensure that any change resulting would not have occurred in the absence of the treatment strategy. Such an investigation might well have to be designed as a group study, and these are discussed in Chapter 4. However, there are other ways of examining academic performance, and Chapter 6 contains some illustrative examples.

A long term project like this would require considerable planning, and would need to include such features as short term reinforcers, and perhaps the promise of a 'powerful reinforcer' at the end of the treatment. That this is not necessarily an unrealistic project may be appreciated, when one considers the efforts that some pupils will make during their final year in a secondary school, in order to obtain GCE or CSE pass grades.

The Selection of Reinforcers

Selecting an appropriate reinforcer for a pupil is not always the simplest of tasks. Sometimes the choice of a reinforcer shows real ingenuity on the part of a teacher. Yet beneath this ingenuity, there almost certainly lies a careful consideration of sources of information. Let us examine some of these sources.

When a teacher makes the decision to use behaviour modification procedures to help a pupil whose classroom difficulties are of a social nature, he will initially have a good knowledge of the pupil. Not only will he be concerned to pin-point the exact nature of the difficulties, he will also be concerned to see why the difficulties exist. When he makes baseline observations of the pupil's behaviour, he will of necessity be watching the pupil closely and extracting further information.

By the end of the baseline observation period, the teacher may well have a very good idea of what is reinforcing the pupil's behaviour. However, bearing in mind that behaviour needs only to be reinforced intermittently to be maintained, and that a behaviour is seldom maintained by a single reinforcer, the teacher may still be unclear what is reinforcing the behaviour.

At this point, the teacher must hypothesize, and select a potential reinforcer, or reinforcers, based on his knowledge of the pupil, and on his observations of the pupil's behaviour. His hypothesizing should take into account the desirability of using normal classroom reinforcers if these are likely to be effective.

Sometimes, when more artificial forms of reinforcement are required, it is possible to use activities which are themselves of positive value to the pupil. This has already been mentioned in connection with the pupil who liked to read to his teacher. In another case, a pupil who misbehaved frequently, and whose speech was poor, expressed the desire to use a cassette recorder. He was allowed to buy time on the cassette recorder by behaving well in class, and by practising speech with his teacher. He used the cassette recorder to talk to, and to play back his own speech. Other investigations have shown that individual pupils, and indeed whole classes, will improve their behaviour and increase their work output to obtain more time in a selected lesson. These are reinforcers *par excellence*, and they are best identified by discussion with pupils.

In a similar vein, in the study which was quoted earlier (Burns 1978), secondary school pupils, aged eleven to fifteen, were asked to rank in order of priority the incentives they most preferred from a list of twelve. Top of the list for boys and girls was 'A favourable report sent home'. The teachers of these pupils were asked independently to rank the incentives in order of their effectiveness. 'A favourable report sent home' was not put at the top of their list. It was placed fifth by male teachers, and seventh by female teachers.

The difference between the pupils' ranking and the teachers' ranking was not restricted to 'A favourable report sent home'. Throughout the whole list there were many differences. Of course, this doesn't necessarily mean that the teachers were misperceiving their pupils' reactions to incentives, since each group was being asked a different question. However, it does lend support to the suggestion that asking a pupil what he would like to do, or to receive, can yield valuable information, as was seen in the case of Teddy and the model cars (Chapter 1, page 14).

In summary, there are three potential sources of information which can be used to identify what might be reinforcing to a pupil. These are: (a) the teacher's knowledge of the pupil, (b) the teacher's observation of the pupil, and (c) the pupil's expression of his likes and dislikes.

Concluding Comments

The general aim of this chapter has been to show how teachers can relate the general theory of behaviour modification to their own classroom practices. To set this in its proper context, it has been necessary to outline briefly some of the ways in which schools normally use rewards and punishments. In addition, to ensure that real issues are adequately covered, there has been some discussion of the use of punishment, and of the implication which the organization of the secondary school has for the practice of behaviour modification.

In general, however, the chapter illustrates the many decisions a teacher must take when he wishes to use behaviour modification procedures. Some guidelines have been provided, but in the final analysis, it is the teacher who must make the decisions.

Chapter 4

Measurement and Design

Measurement is fundamental to the practice of behaviour modification. It supplies the major source of evidence upon which teachers make decisions. If a teacher uses a behaviour modification procedure to change a pupil's behaviour, and does not include any form of measurement, he will have to rely on his memory when evaluating the results; and since memory can be unreliable, it is quite likely that the evaluation will be tentative and limited. Moreover, if small changes in behaviour occur, they are virtually impossible to detect without measurement.

The teacher who measures accurately can look back at his recordings, and can reflect on any pattern of change which may have occurred in a pupil's behaviour. He can directly compare the recordings of today with those of last week, or even of last month, and consequently he can make his decisions against a background of detailed evidence.

Measurement in behaviour modification is not difficult. It may involve counting the number of times a particular behaviour occurred during a certain time period, or noting the time it takes a pupil to complete a certain task, but it does not involve any complicated statistical procedures.

At this point, the reader may feel that he is about to become the victim of a confidence trick, in view of the number of pages he sees stretching out ahead of him on measurement. If measurement is that simple, what are all those pages about? The short answer is that different behaviours require different forms of measurement, for example, measuring the 'out of seat' behaviour of a pupil who seems to wander continually around the classroom, is very different from measuring the behaviour of a pupil who is learning to read.

This chapter is divided into three parts: the first part is concerned with measurement, the second part is a discussion of the ways in which behaviour modification investigations are designed, and the final part is concerned with the examination of results.

Measurement

Defining Behaviour

Throughout the text so far, there has been continual reference to the defining of behaviour. This is a necessary first step in measurement. In normal discussion, pupils are often described in such terms as 'a willing lad, but a real nuisance at times', 'very timid and shy', or 'a real trouble-maker'. Such descriptions may be very appropriate, but they do not lend themselves to accurate observation. If a teacher sets out to observe how often a pupil is a 'nuisance', he will find himself continually having to make decisions about whether certain behaviours can or cannot be categorized as 'nuisance' behaviours. Over a period, the accuracy of his observations will suffer because of his changing criteria of what 'nuisance' behaviour involves; when he wishes to discuss his results with other teachers, he will find that he has to explain how his criteria of 'nuisance' behaviour have been established.

This difficulty can be avoided by an initial, careful definition of behaviours to be observed. A pupil who is a nuisance may talk to other pupils when he ought to be working, and may shout out to the teacher when the teacher is himself talking. Alternatively, he may ramble about the classroom when he is supposed to be working at his desk, and seemingly without intention, may nudge other pupils *en route*. These are behaviours which can be easily measured if they are carefully defined.

It is very important to make any definition of behaviour as complete as possible, so that consistency of measurement can be achieved. If, for example, 'being out of seat' is to be observed, the definition ought to specify whether it includes standing out of the seat, yet still being in contact with it, and standing up whilst working at the desk. If the definition neither includes nor excludes such potential behaviours, there is a real danger that in subsequent observations they will not always be correctly classified. This may seem pernickety, but it is no more so than the use of a marking scheme aimed at accurate scoring of pupils' academic output.

Ways of Measuring Behaviour

Measurement by Traces

Behaviours which occur in classrooms are transient, although sometimes they leave a lasting, clearly observable trace. These traces are most clearly seen as the academic products of the pupils, for example, test results and work completed, but they also exist as school records.

ACADEMIC PRODUCTS This form of measurement is generally used in schools when teachers mark exercises and examination papers. It is used in a similar way in behaviour modification, for example, in the case of 'Teddy', which was described in Chapter 1, the number of words written during English lessons was counted. Tests of spelling, reading, and achievement in various subjects, can all be used when a teacher is seeking to modify academic progress. Such tests can provide the teacher with both baseline and final levels of performance, against which he can evaluate his method of treatment. Moreover, they can be adapted to provide intermediate indications of the progress of treatment.

RECORDS A pupil's records can be very useful to a teacher when he is seeking to understand any difficulties the pupil may experience in school. When a teacher begins to consider using behaviour modification techniques to alleviate these difficulties, information on the pupil's previous school experience, adjustment and achievement levels can be of considerable help.

Additionally, in the long term, an examination of the pupil's subsequent record can yield useful information on the lasting results of treatment. Such records may be difficult to obtain, but they should be sought out as part of any final evaluation.

Measurement of Transitory Behaviours

Many of the behaviours with which teachers are concerned leave little lasting trace. These include such behaviours as, 'disturbing other pupils', 'shouting out', 'not answering the teacher's questions', and 'not lining up properly'. Such behaviours can best be measured by one or other of the following methods.

FREQUENCY RECORDING A teacher is using frequency recording when he makes a record of each time a behaviour occurs. This is usually a tally on a sheet of paper, although it could be the movement of a bead on a string, or the click of a golf-stroke counter. Whichever method is selected depends very much on the teacher's personal preference, and the ease with which the count can be taken.

A behaviour which is amenable to frequency recording must fulfil two basic requirements. It must be infrequent and it must be of short duration. The behaviour must be infrequent so that the teacher's attention is not over-taxed, and it must be brief if records are to be useful. If a behaviour occurs perhaps once a day for long periods of time, frequency recording will yield little of value. Similarly, if a behaviour occurs two or three times a day for varying periods of time, frequency recording may yield very misleading results, since a treatment which reduced the frequency of a behaviour might not reduce the overall duration of the behaviour.

Frequency recording is probably the simplest method of recording for teachers to use, and it is particularly appropriate for behaviours like 'interrupts the teacher', 'pushes other pupils' and 'number of sums completed'. It will be recalled that this method of recording provided a good measure of Peter's 'bouncing behaviour' (Chapter 1, page 11). However, frequency recording is less appropriate for behaviours of potentially long duration, for example, 'has conversation with pupil in neighbouring desk'.

DURATION RECORDING A teacher is using duration recording when he measures the length of time a behaviour takes. This form of measurement can be very useful for certain behaviours, for example, recording the time a pupil takes to settle down to work after instructions have been given, or noting for how long a pupil will work at a set task.

Suppose, for example, that a teacher is concerned about the time a pupil takes to settle down to written work set in class. The teacher could record the time which elapses between the instruction to begin work, and the pupil commencing to write in his book. A record of this might be kept, as shown in Table 1.

Lesson in which work is set	Eng Mon	Maths Mon	Hist Mon	Eng Tues	Geog Tues	Maths Wed	Eng Thurs	Maths Thurs	Eng Fri
Time taken to begin work (secs)	290	115	34	415	45	210	650	170	315

Table 1

If the teacher records not only the duration of the behaviour, but also the kind of lesson and the day, further light may be shed on the pupil's behaviour, so that in the example given here, it is seen that the pupil seems to take a longer time settling down to English than to Maths, and takes a relatively short time settling down to History and Geography. There may well be a clue to subsequent treatment in such a record.

There are, however, certain difficulties inherent in this method of recording. The teacher has to time the behaviour, and whereas looking at a watch or a strategically placed clock poses little difficulty, the need to observe continually the behaviour of one pupil does pose difficulties. When the teacher has other tasks to perform, he may not be able to afford the luxury of watching one member of his class. It may be possible to do this if the behaviour occurs at certain, infrequent, predictable times, but in other circumstances the teacher's attention may be overloaded. If, however, a whole class is to be observed, the difficulties are slightly alleviated, since all the pupils will be watched, say, until they settle down to work. Even so, it is difficult to time durations if the behaviours of concern occur at all frequently.

INTERVAL RECORDING Interval recording is a technique which can be used to give a clear indication of both the frequency and the duration of a behaviour. It also possesses a degree of flexibility, so that the teacher can adjust the timing of his recordings to meet the demands on his attention.

Consider the following example, in which a teacher used interval recording to measure the 'shouting out', and 'talking to other pupils' behaviours of a member of his class. He made out a record sheet divided into equal intervals, each interval representing ten seconds. He selected the first ten seconds of every minute to be his recording intervals. This left him free to watch the other pupils for fifty seconds during each minute. Whenever the pupil 'shouted out', or 'talked to other pupils', during a ten second interval of direct observation, a tally was made on the record sheet as shown in Table 2. The pupil's behaviour during the other fifty seconds of each minute was not recorded.

	1	2	3	4	5	6	7	8	9	10	11	12	13	14	15
Shouts out	/	/				/		/			/				
Talks to others		/		/							/			/	

Intervals

Table 2

In this way, the teacher was able to observe during how many intervals the pupil shouted out or talked. The record shows that the pupil was 'shouting out' at some time during the first, second, sixth, eighth and eleventh intervals, and was 'talking' at some time during the second, fourth, eleventh and fourteenth intervals. This gives a good estimate of his 'shouting out' and 'talking' behaviour.

Whilst the length of time between the intervals can be adjusted to reduce the stress on the teacher's attention, and to allow him to pay attention to other pupils, there is always the problem that the teacher must remember when an interval starts, and when it finishes. This makes interval recording a difficult method to use for long periods of time, although it could be a valuable method to use for short time periods, particularly when the class is meant to be working and the teacher is seated at his desk.

TIME-SAMPLING Time-sampling requires the teacher to note whether a behaviour is occurring or not, at a number of pre-determined times. It may be, for example, that a teacher seeks to record whether a pupil is 'on task' at five minute intervals. At exactly 5, 10, 15, 20 minutes, and so on, he would look at the pupil and note whether he was 'on task', or not. Behaviour in the intervening times would not be recorded.

A record sheet for time-sampling 'on task' behaviour might look as in Table 3.

Minutes	5	10	15	20	25	30	35	40
Behaviour	+	–	–	–	+	+	–	+

Table 3

The + marks would indicate that the pupil was 'on task' at the observed times, and the – marks that he was not.

Unfortunately, like interval recording, this technique requires the teacher to remember when to record. In addition, unless the behaviour to be recorded is extremely frequent, or of long duration, large time periods between observations, such as are shown in the above example, will result in an inaccurate estimation of actual behaviour occurring. Research by Powell *et al.* (1977) indicates that time-sampling needs to be undertaken as frequently as once per minute to yield an accurate measure of behaviour. Such frequent observation would seem to be impossible for a teacher to undertake over a long time period, although, like interval recording, time-sampling could be usefully employed for a short time when the pupils are working at their desks.

There are, however, ways around this. Merrett and Wheldall (1978) used a cassette recorder which gave an audible ping at pre-set intervals, and whenever the ping sounded the teacher observed and recorded the pupil's behaviour. To avoid the pupil's behaviour becoming synchronized to the pings, they varied the time intervals between the pings. It might be objected that the ping would be unnecessarily intrusive in the classroom, and indeed it might be. However, it ought to be possible to reduce the sound, and place the recorder where only the teacher could hear it.

The reader will probably realize that this method of reminding a teacher when to record could equally well be used in interval recording, and wonder why it was seemingly overlooked. The answer is relatively simple; if such a reminder is to be used, it is best used in time-sampling. If the reminder is heard by the pupils, then adjustments can be made to subsequent behaviour, so that interval recording would become valueless. However, even if the reminder is heard only by the teacher, time-sampling is still the more accurate form of measurement. The weakness inherent in interval recording is that an interval is scored for one instance of a behaviour occurring during an interval. Should more than one instance occur, this is not represented. This means that the more frequently a behaviour occurs, the more likely it is to be under-estimated in the data obtained by interval recording. This weakness is not shared by time-sampling.

General Comments

Measuring a pupil's behaviour may seem to be an onerous task, but it is a very revealing exercise. Whichever method is selected must depend on a variety of features, not least of which are the kinds of behaviour to be observed, the times when these behaviours are likely to occur, and the time the teacher has available to observe and record.

One very successful way of obtaining recordings in the classroom is to enlist the aid of a helper, perhaps a classroom assistant or, alternatively, student teachers from local Colleges or University Departments, who are usually eager to gain classroom experience, and can benefit considerably from such an exercise. When such observers are given sufficient guidance, they can record far more detail than any teacher could hope to obtain whilst he is in charge of a class.

Observer Accuracy

When one person records on his own, there is always a danger that he will be inconsistent, and therefore, inaccurate. For this reason, if it is practical, it is advantageous to have a second observer, at least periodically, with whom to check the accuracy of recording. Provided both observers are very clear about the way in which behaviours are defined, a little practice should ensure that they code the behaviours in the same way.

When accuracy checks are being made, it is important that the second observer has as clear a view of the pupil as possible, and that none of the behaviours to be observed is obscured from him. Both the teacher and the observer must of course record independently, but at the same times.

A careful examination of the recordings made by the teacher and the observer will indicate how closely they agree. However, one ought to take this examination a stage further and calculate the percentage agreement obtained. This is accomplished by means of a simple formula which varies slightly depending upon the method of recording used.

1 When frequency recording has been used, and the teacher has recorded that a pupil 'shouted out', say 25 times in the lesson, and the observer has noted 22 such instances, then percentage agreement would be calculated as follows:

$$\text{Percentage Agreement} = \frac{22 \times 100}{25} \quad 88\%$$

i.e.

$$\text{Percentage Agreement} = \frac{\text{Smaller frequency recorded}}{\text{Larger frequency recorded}} \times 100$$

2 When duration of behaviour is recorded, this formula is amended to:

$$\text{Percentage Agreement} = \frac{\text{Smaller duration recorded}}{\text{Larger duration recorded}} \times 100$$

3 When interval and time-sample recordings are used, the formula becomes:

$$\text{Percentage Agreement} = \frac{\text{Number of agreements}}{\text{Number of agreements} + \text{disagreements}} \times 100$$

For example, if one examines the record sheets (reproduced in Table 4) of a teacher and an observer who were recording 'shouting out' behaviour during ten intervals, it is seen that they agree on 8 intervals and disagree on 2 intervals.

Interval	1	2	3	4	5	6	7	8	9	10
Teacher	/		/	/			/		/	/
Observer	/		/				/	/	/	/

Table 4

Applying the formula:

$$\text{Percentage Agreement} = \frac{8}{8+2} \times 100 = 80\%$$

Calculating the percentage agreement between observers is a very useful way of comparing recording data, and it does give a good indication of accuracy. In practice however, it is quite unusual to attain 100 per cent agreement, and most investigators consider 80 per cent agreement to be satisfactory. Levels below this figure do give cause for concern, and ought to lead to a reconsideration of both the definition of behaviours and of the means of recording.

Design

In this section, the two research designs most commonly used in educational research, correlational studies and group studies, will be briefly discussed, and the reasons why they are not generally appropriate for behaviour modification research will be outlined. Following on from this, the three designs most commonly used in behaviour modification research will be explained.

Correlation Studies

In a correlational study, an investigator seeks to establish the relationship between one variable and another. He might for example set out to examine the relationship between the number of homework exercises submitted by pupils during their final year in a comprehensive school, and the examination results obtained by the pupils. Such research might yield a positive correlation, that is, in general, the more homework submitted, the better the examination result. In a similar manner, an investigator might find a negative correlation between the number of times pupils cause trouble in school, and the number of times their parents attend school 'open-days', that is, in general, the more trouble that is caused by pupils, the less frequently do their parents attend 'open-days'. It must be added, however, that these are merely illustrative examples, and the results of such investigations might yield very different results.

In practice, correlational studies do tend to be addressed to more complex issues, for example, the relationship between personality factors and academic attainment (Entwistle, 1972), and can tease out many relationships between variables. However, the results do not tell the investigator that one variable has caused another. If one takes an extreme example, there would almost certainly be a positive correlation between the size of boys' trousers and their ability to play basketball. Quite obviously, this does not mean that buying larger trousers for a boy will make him a better basketball player. On the other hand, correlational studies can make useful suggestions, and to be fair to investigators who use this approach, no claims are made that one variable causes another.

In addition to not specifying causes of behaviour, correlational studies are concerned with general results. This means that the scores of individual pupils are submerged in a mass of group data, so that overall findings, rather than specific findings are produced.

Behaviour modification research is very different. It is concerned with what causes behaviour, and with individual rather than with group results. For these reasons, behaviour modifiers tend to make little use of correlational studies.

Group Studies

Unlike correlational studies, group studies are concerned with causes. As an illustration, consider an investigation which aims to see if a new method of teaching French is superior to traditional teaching methods. The achievement levels in French of two equally matched groups of pupils could be measured. One group could be taught French by the new method, and the other could be taught by the traditional method. At the end of several months, both groups could be retested by an achievement test of French. The results would indicate whether or not the new method was superior to the traditional method.

This is a very logical procedure, but unfortunately it is not usually possible to arrange the conditions as easily as the illustration indicates. In practice, if different teachers were taking the groups, the results might well be attributable to differences between the teachers. If the same teacher taught both groups, any difference might be due to the teacher's enthusiasm for one method. In addition, it is possible that the receptiveness of the pupils to the teaching methods might depend upon the way in which the pupils have previously been taught, or even upon their intelligence level; that is, the new method might work better than the traditional method with brighter pupils, or vice versa.

Because of these complexities, group studies tend to grow in size, for example, to iron out differences between teachers, a number of groups would have to be taught in the new way by several teachers, and a number of matched groups would have to be taught in the traditional way by several teachers. Likewise, matched groups might be set up of varying educational background, and of varying intelligence levels.

Eventually, it might be possible to specify whether or not the new method of teaching French is superior to the traditional method. However, the conclusion would still be limited by the factors that the research had taken into account.

Whilst group studies can be rather cumbersome, they are concerned with changing conditions in one way or another, and in evaluating the results of change, so that they can be used for examining classroom processes; for example, a group study could be designed to examine the effectiveness of posting classroom rules beside the blackboard. Such studies can yield useful results which can tell us a good deal about the way in which various processes can effect pupils in general.

Behaviour modifiers sometimes use group studies when they wish to examine the results of a particular kind of treatment. However, such investigations give only general results, and the reactions of individual pupils to the treatment have to be ignored. More usually, it is the individual pupil who is the focus of attention in a behaviour modification investigation, and his behaviour may well differ from that of the group.

Behaviour Modification Research

The results of correlational and group studies can be very useful to the teacher when he is concerned with his pupils in general. However, these approaches have less to offer him when he is dealing with the idiosyncrasies of particular pupils. Moreover, because he is concerned primarily with teaching, he is unlikely to have the facilities available to enable him to engage in research of this nature. By contrast, behaviour modification is concerned primarily with individual pupils, and as such it does offer the teacher an opportunity to engage in research within his own classroom.

There are three designs commonly in use: the AB design, which was met in Chapter 1, although it was not named; the ABA design; and the multiple-baseline design.

The AB Design

In this design, the behaviours of concern are clearly defined, and observations are taken throughout the course of the investigation. The A phase involves a series of baseline measurements to determine the extent of the behaviour to be treated. At the start of the B phase, treatment begins, and continues throughout the phase. To put it in more familiar terms, the A phase is the baseline, the B phase is the treatment phase.

The results of such an investigation may best be appreciated by plotting a graph. In the case of Frank, for example (Chapter 1), it was stated that the behaviours which concerned his teacher were reduced from between 5 and 6 instances per observation session before treatment, to between 1 and 2 such instances by the end of the fourth week of treatment. When the day-by-day changes in Frank's behaviour were plotted, the resulting graph approximated to the form shown in Figure 1.

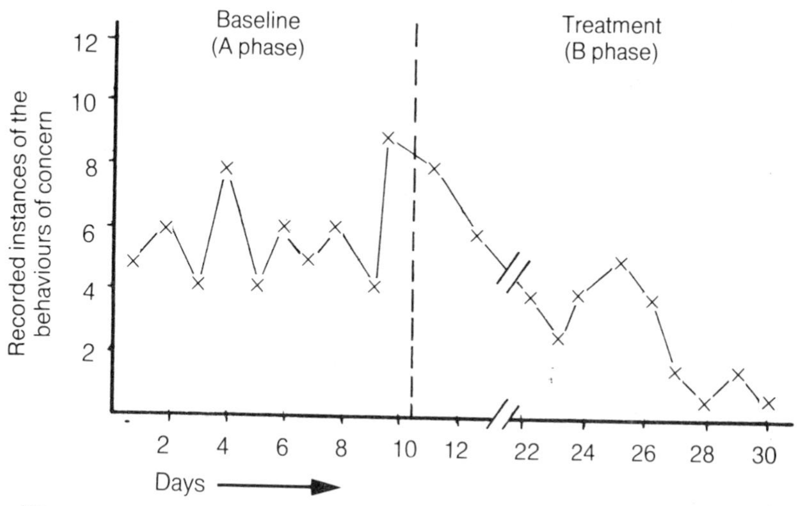

Figure 1

This design has, however, attracted some criticism, which is mainly centred around two contentions. These are that the design doesn't really tell us what would have occurred if treatment had not been applied, and that the ostensible results of treatment may have been caused by some alternative, unidentified factor which has intruded during the treatment phase.

These are serious weaknesses from a methodological point of view, and in an effort to eliminate these weaknesses, many investigators have used the ABA design.

The ABA Design

This design is an extension of the AB design, and adds a third phase (A) which is a repeat of the initial baseline phase. In other words, after treating the pupil, the teacher withdraws the treatment, and reverts to his original way of handling the pupil. Had an

ABA design been used in the treatment of Frank, and if the investigation had demonstrated that Frank's behaviour had reverted to his baseline level of performance during the final phase, the resulting graph would have illustrated this change has shown in Figure 2.

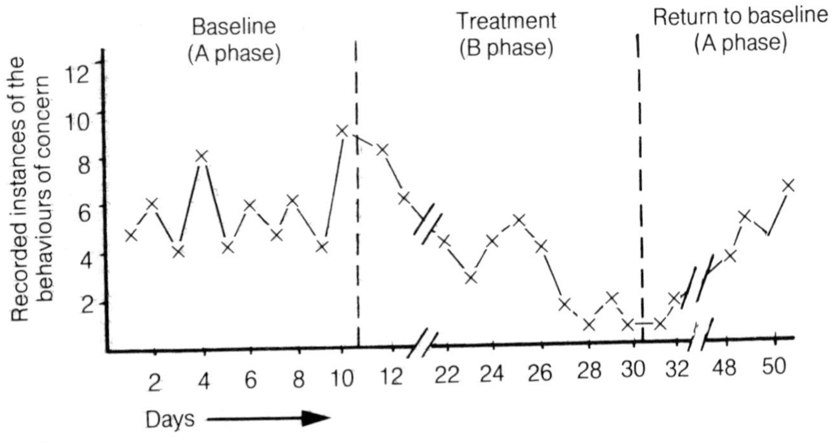

Figure 2

From a methodological point of view, this seems to be an improvement on the AB design, since it can show more clearly whether treatment has had an effect. If the treatment is producing a change in behaviour, then the change ought to be seen in the treatment phase (B), and not in either of the baseline phases (A). If the treatment phase and the subsequent withdrawal phase show no discernible difference, yet both show an improvement in behaviour, then it must be assumed that the treatment has had no effect, and that some other, unidentified factor has produced the change. This is the reasoning behind the ABA design.

Although this design may seem to be a methodological advance on the AB design, it does not in fact stand up to close examination. In practice it can be objected to as undesirable, and theoretically, it possesses its own weaknesses. The design is undesirable from an educational point of view because it ends in a return to baseline conditions, and deprives the pupil of the full benefits of treatment. No teacher wishes to improve a pupil's behaviour and then let it deteriorate again, simply in order to demonstrate that the treatment has been effective.

From a theoretical point of view, the procedure seems to be almost impossible to follow. It would be extremely difficult for a teacher to revert to his original handling of a pupil, even if he should wish to do so, following an apparently successful treatment phase. In addition, the design makes the assumption that the pupil's behaviour is so malleable that it will adapt itself to the teacher's behaviour across the various phases, without any generalization occurring.

The Multiple-Baseline Design

This design is a little more complex than the two which have been previously discussed. However, it does allow the investigator to demonstrate that a treatment has been effective, and it does not involve any procedures which might be considered to be undesirable.

The multiple-baseline design requires that the investigator takes baseline measures of three or more independent behaviours, and then applies treatment to the behaviours in sequence. Whilst the design may be used with different behaviours from one pupil, it can also be applied to the same behaviour from one pupil in different situations, and to the same behaviour from different pupils in one situation. A graphical representation of an investigation using this design is shown on page 76 (Figure 4).

DIFFERENT BEHAVIOURS FROM ONE PUPIL As an example, consider a teacher who is concerned about a pupil whose unwanted behaviour can be subsumed into three categories: 'shouting out', 'talking to other pupils', and 'pulling faces at other pupils'. The teacher takes baseline recordings of all three behaviours until he obtains an accurate estimate of their occurrence. This completed, he applies his treatment strategy, perhaps the use of tokens, to one of the behaviours. When this behaviour is clearly improving, and the other behaviours are not changing, he then applies the treatment to a second behaviour as well as to the first. Finally, when both these behaviours are improving, and the third behaviour remains unchanged, he applies the treatment to all three behaviours. Should all three behaviours improve during this final stage, the multiple-baseline design has been successfully applied.

These results would be very convincing evidence that it was the treatment which was producing the improvement, since the improvement of each behaviour only occurred when the behaviour was treated. It would be most unlikely that any extraneous factor could have affected the behaviours only when treatment was being applied.

This design does not require any withdrawal of treatment. It merely requires that the investigator introduces his treatment in a progressive manner. This makes the design very appropriate for educational practice.

THE SAME PUPIL IN DIFFERENT SITUATIONS A similar procedure can be followed with one pupil in different situations, when, for example, a teacher is concerned about a pupil's behaviour in the classroom, in the playground, and in the school dining room. One troublesome behaviour, for example, physical aggression towards other pupils, could be recorded in all three situations, and a multiple-baseline procedure could be carried out to see if a particular form of treatment would be successful.

DIFFERENT PUPILS IN THE SAME SITUATION If a teacher wished to find out whether a certain treatment would improve a particular behaviour which characterized a group of pupils, he could examine this by using a multiple-baseline design. The behaviour of all the pupils could be recorded, and the pupils could be subsequently treated in sequence.

In general, the multiple-baseline design is a very useful and flexible technique to use in behaviour modifications research, but it does have one inherent difficulty. The behaviours which are to be treated do need to be independent of one another, so that each can be treated separately. It is a little confusing when for example, treating a pupil's 'shouting out' reduces this behaviour, and also reduces another behaviour which is not being treated. In practice of course, this would probably be welcomed by a teacher, but the results would be less welcome if treating 'shouting out' exacerbated another behaviour.

Such confusion occurs when behaviours are interdependent. For example, if a teacher was concerned with 'out of seat' behaviour, 'talking to neighbours' and 'playing with objects on the desk', he might well find that the successful treatment of 'out of seat' behaviour was accompanied by an increase in the other two untreated behaviours, presumably because the pupil would be spending more time in his seat, and would consequently have more time available for 'in-seat' misbehaviours.

There are, however, two ways in which the teacher can minimize the likelihood of obtaining such results. Before recording, he can exclude those behaviours which appear to be interdependent, and later, he can scrutinize the baseline recordings to see if a change in one behaviour is accompanied by a change in another behaviour. If, for example, he has been recording the 'shouting out' behaviour of three pupils, he might find that the 'shouting out' of one pupil tends to be accompanied by the 'shouting out' of another. In the circumstances, treating one pupil's behaviour is likely to have an effect on the behaviour of the other pupil.

Concluding Comments on Behaviour Modification Designs

It may be a little disheartening for the reader to find that there are some design difficulties in behaviour modification. However, this is a feature of educational research which afflicts everyone. No matter how carefully, or elaborately a piece of research is planned, there are always weaknesses which can be detected. These weaknesses can be minimized, but they cannot be eradicated.

Investigations do have to be carefully designed if their results are to be of value. However, the care taken in designing an investigation depends upon the question which the investigator is seeking to answer. If a teacher wishes to see whether behaviour modification procedures will work in his own classroom, then a simple AB design might well be appropriate. Should his results indicate that the treatment was successful, he may have a sneaking feeling that some factor other than the treatment could have produced the results, but in practice this probably will not cause too much concern since the pupil has improved. If he continues to use behaviour modification procedures, he will probably become very skilled in the recognition and use of factors which can change the behaviour of his pupils.

One of the most important points to emerge from the discussion of behaviour modification designs is the need for careful baseline recording of behaviour. It was mentioned in Chapter I that teachers may feel impatient when taking lengthy baselines, and that a baseline is best continued until any behaviour observed 'steadies down'. Likewise, a deteriorating baseline should cause treatment to be brought forward, whereas a steadily improving baseline ought to cause the onset of treatment to be delayed, in order to see if the 'problem' vanishes. In addition to these considerations, the baseline needs to be carefully examined if a number of behaviours are being observed. Should the behaviours appear to be independent of one another, a multiple-baseline design could be carried out. Should the behaviours appear to be interdependent, the use of the AB design would be more appropriate. The decision of which design to use can profitably be delayed until the end of the baseline recording phase.

Finally, let it be added that the would-be investigator should not be too fastidious in his consideration of a design and a method of recording, otherwise he runs the risk of becoming completely incapacitated by the complexities involved and by his own limited resources. He should make careful decisions in the light of his own limited resources and then proceed with his investigation.

Examining Results

The Use of Graphs

Behaviour modifiers have always found graphs to be useful ways of representing results. When a graph is properly constructed, the implications of the data can be more readily appreciated by examining the graph, than by examining the data which are presented in a table.

Consider Figure 3, which is a representation of the baseline recordings taken of three behaviours from a pupil. The graph shows quite clearly, and very rapidly, just how the number of incidents of each behaviour varied during the course of ten days.

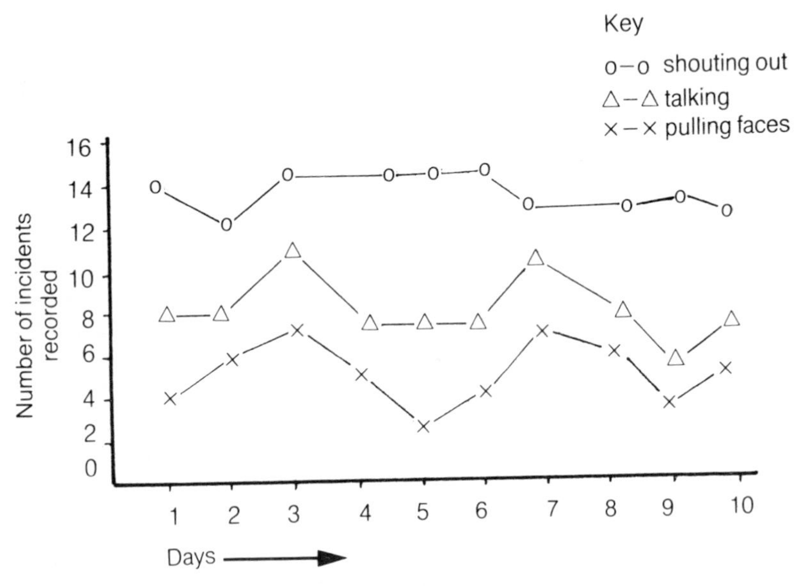

Figure 3, *showing the number of incidents of behaviour recorded during a ten day baseline recording phase*

Alternatively, one might examine the actual results obtained, as detailed in Table 5.

What seems evident from a glance at the graph is certainly not evident from a glance at the table. Apart from seeing that 'shouting out' occurs most frequently, and that 'pulling faces' occurs the least frequently, there is an obvious relationship between 'talking' and 'pulling faces'. Both behaviours display a similar pattern of results, and this would be difficult to see by a mere scrutiny of the

	number of incidents recorded									
Shouting out	14	12	14	14	14	14	12	12	13	12
Talking	8	8	11	8	8	8	10	8	6	7
Pulling faces	4	6	7	4	3	4	7	6	4	5
Day	1	2	3	4	5	6	7	8	9	10

***Table 5**, showing the number of incidents of behaviour recorded during a ten day baseline recording phase*

data in Table 5. And, incidentally, because of the interdependence of 'talking' and 'pulling faces', this indicates that a multiple-baseline design would not be suitable if these behaviours were to be treated.

In a similar way, the entire course of treatment can be plotted graphically. Consider Figure 4, which shows the successful use of a multiple-baseline design (page 76).

Quite clearly, Figure 4 incorporates far more detail than did Figure 3, and therefore requires more scrutiny. However, a careful examination of the graphs shows that:

1. There is no evidence that the behaviours are interdependent.
2. When 'talking' was treated, the number of recorded incidents of 'talking' diminished, whilst the untreated behaviours showed no discernible change.
3. When 'talking' and 'shouting out' were treated, the number of recorded incidents of both diminished, whilst the untreated behaviour, 'doodling', continued at its previous level.
4. When all the behaviours were treated, they all improved.

All of this information can be gleaned by a careful examination of the graphs. The Chinese proverb, 'One picture is worth a thousand words', is very appropriate here.

One question that this discussion of graphs raises is, What do we look for when we wish to see if a behaviour has improved? To answer this question, we must look at two aspects of a graph, the level and the slope. When a treatment is first put into practice it might be accompanied by a change in level, as Figure 5a illustrates, or it might not, as Figure 5b illustrates (page 77).

Each of these graphs indicates that the treatment is improving behaviour (presuming it is a behaviour that the investigator seeks to decrease), but one treatment has had a more instantaneous and static effect than the other. It might well be, for example, that the treatment represented in Figure 5a has been introduced as a

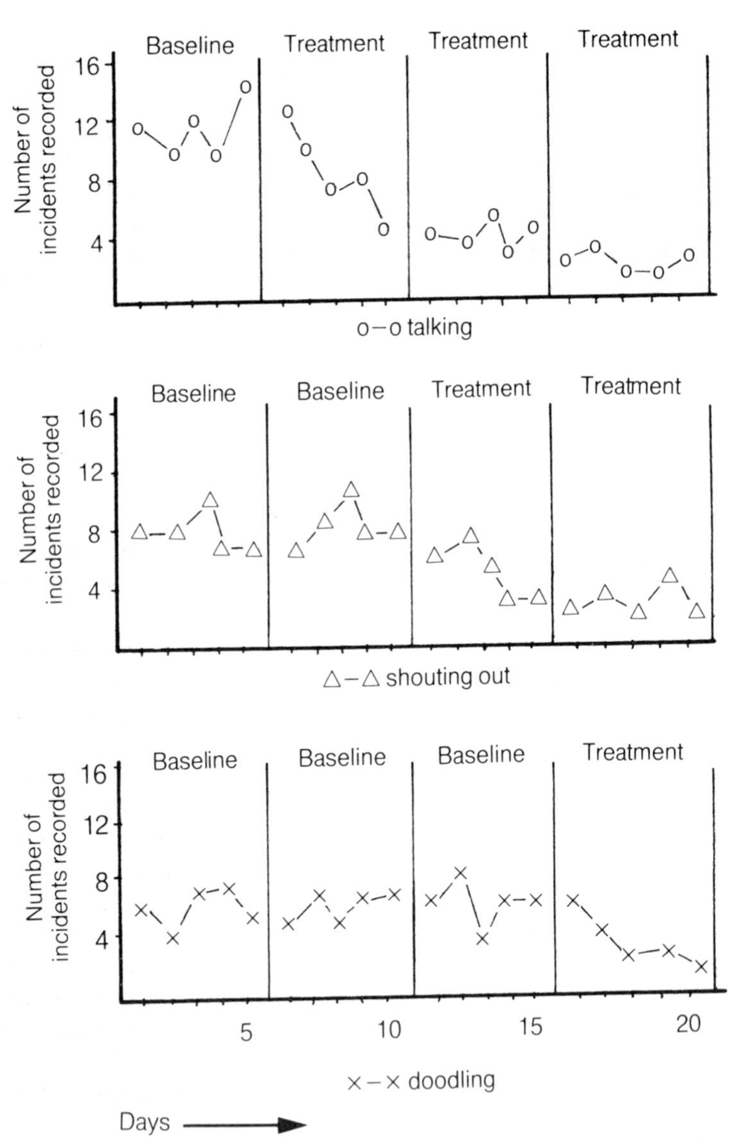

***Figure 4,** showing the number of incidents recorded during the course of an investigation which used a multiple-baseline design*

contract which the pupil has immediately sought to fulfil, whilst the treatment represented in Figure 5b has been a more subtle treatment introduced by the teacher without prior explanation to the pupil. There are, of course, all kinds of permutations of slope and level that could occur when a treatment is put into practice,

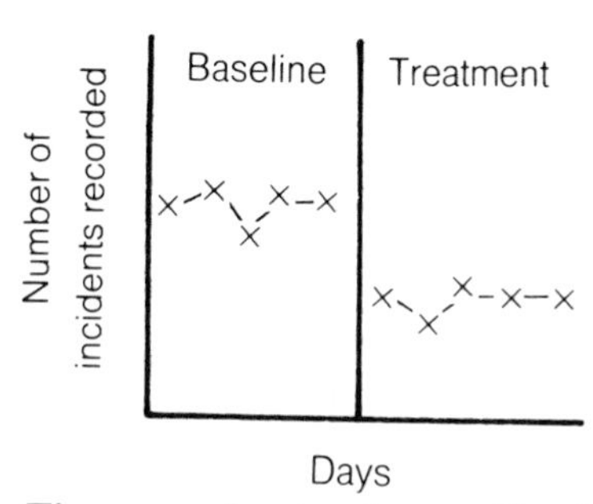

Figure 5a, *showing change of level and not of slope*

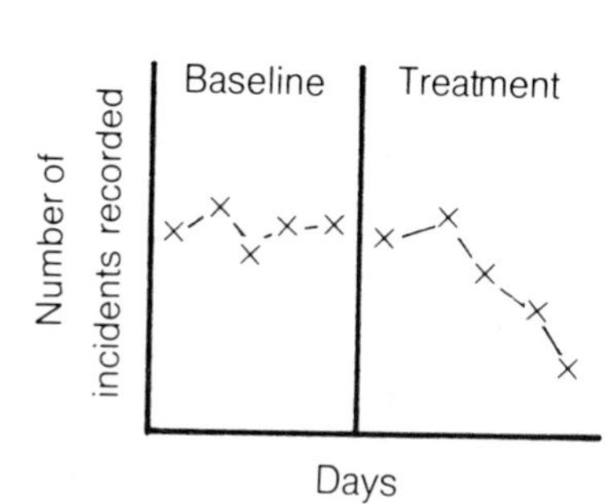

Figure 5b, *showing change of slope and not of level*

and a careful analysis of these is required as part of a continuing evaluation of the success of treatment.

Another question which has not been directly answered as yet, although it has been alluded to before, is, 'How long ought the various phases to be?' To answer this question it is necessary to consider baseline and treatment phases separately.

In a sense, the answer depends upon the time at the investigator's disposal. However, supposing he is eager to treat a behaviour as soon as possible, what he will really want to know is how short a baseline can reasonably be. The answer is a minimum of three separate observations, which when plotted on a graph can establish a trend in the data. If the points show great variability, it is necessary to do more observing, or even to re-examine the behaviour selected and its definition. Even if the behaviour is not variable, it is better to have more than three observations in a baseline record, but if time is limited, three may suffice.

During the treatment phase, recordings can cease when the behaviour 'steadies down' at the level required by the investigator. Should it not reach this level, some other form of treatment may well be necessary. In the long term, of course, it is desirable to re-introduce recording to check that the behaviour has not deteriorated.

Finally, it needs to be mentioned that examining graphs can often yield unexpected insights into a pupil's behaviour. Sometimes, for example, behaviour is seen to vary in a cyclic pattern, and it may be possible to relate the behaviour to specific events, like Friday afternoon misbehaviour, although alternatively, there may be factors contributing to a cyclic pattern of which the teacher will be unaware. However, at the very least, a cyclic pattern does sensitize the teacher to expect different levels of behaviour at different times.

The Interpretation of Results

The most accurate method of interpreting the results of a behaviour modification investigation involves a careful examination of what has been recorded. There is sometimes the temptation to summarize data for ease of interpretation, but this can easily lead to unwarranted assumptions and subsequent inaccurate evaluation.

Examine the data shown in Table 6.

Recorded incidents	12	10	10	12	8	10	8	14	12	8	10	6	4	0	2
Day	1	2	3	4	5	6	7	8	9	10	11	12	13	14	15
	Baseline phase							Treatment phase							

Table 6, *showing the number of incidents of 'talking' recorded during a behaviour modification investigation*

If the investigator summarizes these data and says that during the baseline phase, the behaviour occurred an average of 10 times per recording session, and that this occurrence dropped to an average of 7 times per recording session after treatment, he is being accurate in a mathematical sense, but is he accurately representing the course of treatment? The summary says nothing about the stability of the baseline, ignores the change in level when treatment is introduced, and finally, says nothing about the progressive effects of treatment.[1]

Alternatively, an investigator might be tempted to use percentages to communicate his results. Suppose that in the investigation, each observation session had comprised 50 time-samples, that is at 50 pre-set times per day the pupil had been observed, and whether or not he was 'talking' had been recorded. The investigator, in consequence, might reasonably deduce that during the baseline the pupil 'talked' an average of 10 times per 50 observations, that is, 20 per cent of the time he was observed, and that by

[1] The more statistically sophisticated reader might well be tempted to use statistical procedures like the 't' or 'F' test to compare baseline data with treatment phase data. Whilst these are inappropriate for the reasons given, they are also statistically invalid for the data in Table 6, since such tests assume an independence of error components. In a typical behaviour modification investigation such as this, successive observations are usually correlated, and error components are not independent.

the end of the treatment, that is, during the last day, he 'talked' 4 per cent of the time he was observed. Again, this is accurate mathematically, but it is not accurate to go a step further, and say that his rate of 'talking' was reduced from 20 per cent to 4 per cent, because his actual 'talking' rate was not measured. What was measured was his 'talking' rate for the times observed. In addition, of course, percentages derived from small numbers can be misleading.

Of the four basic methods of recording used in behaviour modification research – frequency, duration, interval recording and time-sampling – the one which can pose the most difficulty of interpretation is interval recording.

Suppose an investigator treats a pupil who 'shouts out', and that he records during twenty 15-second intervals per recording session. The data obtained could be presented in Table 7.

Number of intervals in which the behaviour was recorded	15	16	14	18	12	15	10	8	7	3
Day	1	2	3	4	5	6	7	8	9	10
	Baseline phase					Treatment phase				

Table 7, *showing the number of intervals during which 'shouting out' was recorded*

When these data are scrutinized, it appears evident that the 'shouting out' behaviour has been considerably reduced during the treatment phase. However, even if one heeds the warnings about summarizing data, and sticks with the data presented, there is a danger inherent in these data, since it must be remembered that during interval recording, only one instance of behaviour has to occur within an interval for that interval to be scored. Consequently, for a frequently occurring, short-duration behaviour, it is likely that the results will contain a measure of underestimation, since more than one instance of the behaviour could have occurred in some of the recording intervals. Moreover, this underestimation is more likely to occur when the behaviour rate is high rather than low. During the fourth day of the baseline phase for example, there were 18 intervals during which 'shouting out' was recorded. However, it is very unlikely that the pupil only 'shouted out' 18 times during the twenty 15-second intervals that were observed. During some of the intervals he may well have 'shouted out' several times. Contrast this with the final day of treatment, when 3 intervals recorded 'shouting out'. The actual incidence of 'shouting out' is unlikely to have been very much more.

This means that when the data are plotted, as in Figure 6, the shape of the graph can be misleading, since it is likely that the actual effectiveness of the treatment is greater than it would appear to be from a scrutiny of the graph.

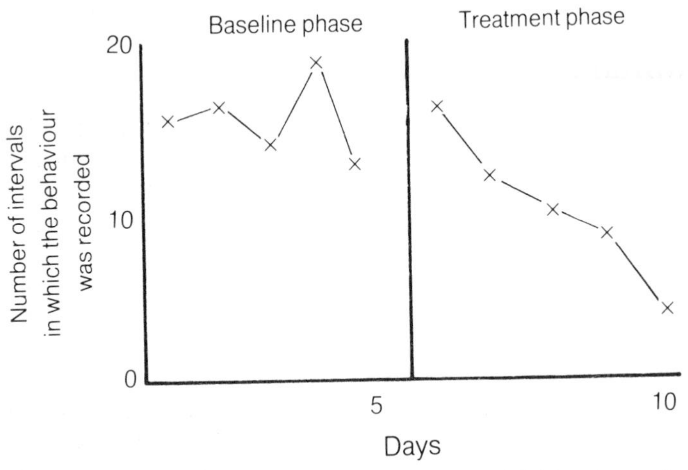

***Figure 6,** showing the number of intervals during which 'shouting out' was recorded*

The same reasoning can be used when one examines data from an investigation in which the behaviour of a pupil is increased, for example, when a very quiet pupil is being helped to interact with the teacher and with his peers. Once again, a graphical representation of data obtained by interval recording is likely to underestimate the effectiveness of treatment.

Fortunately, this complication does not occur with frequency and duration recording, or with time-sampling, so that the interpretation of data obtained by these methods is more straightforward. If frequency recording is used for short-duration behaviours, and if duration recording is used for periodic long-duration behaviours, interpretation of data presents no difficulties. Time-sampling is rather different, since it records only a sample of behaviour, and the investigator has always to be cautious when generalizing from a sample. Provided, however, that the time-sample is taken as frequently as once per minute, an accurate estimate can be obtained of the actual behaviour occurring.

Concluding Comments on the Interpretation of Results

Although this brief excursion into some of the problems involved in the interpretation of results may have seemed a little complicated, it has been undertaken in order to indicate the potential dangers that can afflict the investigator when he strays too far from his data. There is no substitute for a concise presentation of results, and a carefully considered examination of an accurate, unprocessed, graphical representation.

Summary

The various forms of measurement used in behaviour modification research have been described. Whilst these forms of measurement are relatively easy to apply, it has been seen that there are important considerations to be taken into account before deciding which form to adopt in a particular situation.

The three basic designs most commonly used have been discussed, and some guidance has been included as an aid in the selection of an appropriate design.

Finally, there has been a consideration of some of the problems attendant upon the examination of results. Here, the appropriate use of graphs has been emphasised, together with some comments on the accurate representation and interpretation of recorded data.

Chapter 5

Setting up an Investigation

In the first four chapters, sufficient material has been presented to enable the reader to design, conduct and evaluate a classroom investigation. However, the material has been presented in a variety of contexts, and needs now to be structured into a workable programme.

To avoid unnecessary repetition, the early parts of the chapter are written as if to one teacher undertaking a behaviour modification investigation in his own classroom. However, groups of teachers who wish to conduct such an investigation should experience little difficulty in adapting the comments to their own situations (see Chapter 3, pages 51–3).

The chapter is in two parts. In the first part, guidelines are given to facilitate the setting up of an investigation. There is little that should be new to the reader in these guidelines. They are very closely related to the earlier section which outlined the decisions a teacher has to make when using behaviour modification techniques (pages 49–51). However, for the sake of clarity, this outline is extended and organized into a series of steps. The second part of the chapter consists of a discussion aimed at elaborating some of the more important features of an investigation.

Guidelines for Setting up an Investigation

Because the previous chapters have included considerable discussion of the theoretical background and practical implications involved in each of these steps, it is neither appropriate nor practical to reintroduce this detail here. Accordingly, the steps are presented in note form.

A *First Considerations*

1 A pupil should be selected who experiences difficulties in the classroom. These difficulties should be such that they interfere with his learning, and/or the learning of others. The difficulties may be social or academic.
2 Examine the curriculum and decide whether the difficulties

can be alleviated by a more appropriate choice of curriculum material. If not, proceed to step 3.

3 Define the behaviours of concern in as much detail as possible.

4 Decide how best the behaviours of concern may be measured: by frequency, duration or interval recording, or by time-sampling (see pages 60–4).

5 Consider when the behaviours are likely to occur, and consequently decide when to take measurements.

6 Examine the list of behaviours selected and consider how many can be measured, given the conditions in your classroom. If necessary, reduce the list to those behaviours most central to the pupil's difficulties.

B *The Baseline*

7 Systematically observe the pupil at predetermined times and, if possible, plot the results graphically. If a reasonably steady, level pattern of behaviour is observed, the baseline can be discontinued after two weeks. Should great variability of behaviour be observed, extend the baseline for a further week, to see if a steady pattern emerges.

A baseline which shows a rapid deterioration in behaviour should be terminated quickly and treatment introduced. A baseline which shows a steady improvement should be extended to see if the pupil's difficulties vanish.

8 At the end of the baseline period, reflect on what you have learned about the pupil's behaviour. Examine any hypotheses you may have formed, and seek to turn these into a treatment strategy. Should no hypotheses have emerged, analyze what is maintaining the pupil's behaviour.

For a disruptive pupil, consider what is reinforcing the 'unwanted' behaviour, and why he is not being reinforced for appropriate behaviour – for example, does he gain your attention when he wanders about the room, and lose your attention when he sits working at his desk? Decide which behaviour ought to be reinforced, and how reinforcement may best be given.

For an overly reserved pupil whose difficulty lies in a lack of appropriate behaviour, and who may not show any overt 'unwanted' behaviour, consider how best to introduce a subtle means of reinforcement, perhaps utilizing a form of shaping (page 34), or a 'behavioural trap' (page 19).

C *The Treatment*

9 Decide on a treatment strategy which is as close to your normal classroom practice as possible. Select a more artificial strategy only if you feel convinced of its necessity.

10 Whatever the treatment decided upon, include the introduction of rules to the whole class, unless this is felt to be clearly inappropriate for the kind of pupil involved.

11 If the treatment selected involves anything other than attention and praise, for example, tokens or a contract, make sure that attention and praise are paired with the treatment.

12 Give some thought at this stage to the way in which the treatment, if successful, can be faded out later. Avoid, if possible, any treatment which is not amenable to fading out – unless, of course, you wish to introduce a new, enduring system within the classroom.

13 Put the treatment into practice, and continue to observe the pupil's behaviour in exactly the same way as during the baseline period.

14 Constantly scrutinize the data, and examine initial reactions to treatment. Remember the possibility of the 'storm before the calm', but if behaviour reaches an unacceptable level, terminate the treatment. Within a week of the start of treatment it should be possible to decide whether the treatment is being effective.

15 If treatment is ineffective, return to step 8. If treatment is successful, continue until the behaviour is much improved, and you feel that it is time to begin fading out the treatment.

D *Final Considerations*

16 Fading out of treatment must be introduced. When social reinforcement has been the primary means of treatment, this involves the gradual introduction of intermittent reinforcement, that is, a gradual spacing out. When a more 'artificial' treatment has been employed, this involves a progressive reduction in the artificial features of the treatment.

17 Continue to observe the pupil and, should any deterioration occur in behaviour, be prepared to adjust the treatment temporarily before fading out is again undertaken.

18 Ensure that the pupil receives appropriate, legitimately earned reinforcement for good behaviour and work, in the same way as do the other normally behaved pupils.

19 Keep a check on the pupil's subsequent behaviour and, if at all possible, find out what you can about his progress in other classes.

Some Elaborations on the Guidelines

The steps which have been outlined may seem to be very sparse, but they are not intended to be complete in themselves. They should, however, act as triggering mechanisms to remind the reader of the numerous points which have been made in the earlier chapters. At the same time, there are certain practical considerations involved in these steps which have not yet been discussed completely, and it is to these considerations that more detailed attention needs to be drawn.

1 *Selecting a Pupil*

(a) It has been mentioned earlier that whole classes may be selected for treatment for certain specific behaviours. Why then should these be excluded from the guidelines? The answer is that behaviour modification is essentially individually based, and it is better to begin gaining experience of the techniques by working with one pupil.
(b) In selecting one pupil for treatment, the teacher may feel that he is ignoring the needs of other pupils. This is not true. Anything the teacher learns in his treatment of one pupil will surely be generalized to his treatment of others. When he has successfully treated one pupil he can select others for systematic treatment.

2 *The Behaviours of Concern*

It is not always easy to define a pupil's difficulties in behavioural terms. And, indeed, sometimes the need to define in behavioural terms can tend to bias the teacher away from what he originally perceived to be the most central aspects of the pupil's difficulties.

A useful way around this problem is to write a 'pen-portrait', a paragraph or two in length, describing the essential nature of the pupil's difficulties. This pen-portrait should suggest categories of behaviour for measurement. Sometimes such a description will lend itself to easy translation into behaviour, for example, when a pupil is described as talking when he should be working, or frequently interrupting the teacher. At other times it will not; for example, a pupil may be described as idle, ill-mannered and attention-seeking, or as restless and incapable of concentrating at a task. In such cases, the teacher must ask himself what it is that the pupil does in the classroom that enables such judgements to be made. When a pen-portrait is examined in such a way, it is usually not difficult to translate the pupil's difficulties into behaviours to observe.

If, for example, the pupil is considered to be idle, or incapable of concentrating, it should be possible to translate these characteristics into 'off-task' behaviour during those parts of lessons in which pupils are meant to be working. If a pupil is considered to be ill-mannered, it may be possible to break this down into such behaviours as 'interrupting the teacher', 'speaking out when not required to do so', and 'interrupting other pupils when they are working'.

For some pupils, that is, those of an overly reserved kind, the teacher may be concerned about behaviours which do *not* occur, for example, 'asking questions', 'raising a hand in answer to a question', and consequently, he may feel that there are no behaviours to observe. However, if these are behaviours which the teacher wishes to see the pupil adopt, then these are the behaviours which should be measured. A score of zero throughout the baseline is a very steady, level rate of responding, against which improvement can be evaluated. In practice, however, when teachers observe such pupils closely, they tend to note more of such behaviour than they had previously estimated.

3 *How and When to Observe*

When a list of behaviours has been drawn up, the teacher has to decide by what method each is best measured, and when each behaviour is likely to occur. In many cases, the decisions he comes to are likely to produce an unrealistic measuring task when combined with his normal teaching, unless he can gain the help of an observer.

There are, however, ways around this dilemma. Very often the behaviours of concern occur during specific parts of lessons, for example, when pupils are meant to be working at their desks, so that observations need not be made during other parts of lessons. If behaviours are of short duration and very frequent, a short period of interval recording or time-sampling could be conducted. For infrequent, short-duration behaviours a simple count could be made, perhaps during a limited time period each day. Behaviours which are of long duration and occur infrequently, but at predictable times, might best be observed by measuring their durations.

The most difficult problem at this stage tends not to be how to gain an estimate of each individual behaviour, but rather how to obtain a measure of a number of behaviours. Unless a convenient way of measuring can be devised which does not unduly interfere with the normal practice of teaching, some of the behaviours will have to remain unmeasured. Which behaviour or behaviours to measure can only be decided by carefully considering the precise nature of the pupil's difficulties, and the extent to which each behaviour on the list reflects these difficulties. It is sometimes useful at this point to combine categories of behaviour, so that, for example, 'interrupts the teacher', 'speaks out when not required to do so', and 'interrupts other pupils when they are working', may be combined into a defined category of 'inappropriate talking'. In this way, the teacher can avoid discarding potentially valuable information, yet can keep the measuring task within reasonable limits.

4 *Other Measures*

All too often, when behaviour modifiers reach the end of the successful treatment of a pupil, they realize that other information would have been valuable. Sometimes this information can be retrieved when it exists in the form of a lasting trace, such as work in class books, or test scores, so that when a teacher successfully treats a pupil's disruptive behaviour, he can also make an evaluation of changes in his academic performance. In other circumstances, however, where transient behaviour is concerned, the teacher may be left in some doubt; in circumstances, for example, when work output is treated and increased without any measure of disruptive behaviour being made.

To avoid having to speculate about such changes, it might be worth including a brief measure of other behaviours of concern at some point early during the baseline, and at some point towards the end of treatment. The value of such information will depend upon how much data is extracted, but even so it will almost certainly be a better guide to progress than relying upon memory.

5 *The Treatment*

It will have been noted that no prescription has been given for treatment. No two pupils are exactly alike, so that in the final analysis, the teacher has to make informed guesses at what will reinforce 'wanted' behaviour, and what needs to be removed from 'unwanted' behaviour.

Whenever possible, it is prudent to bring the rules of the classroom to the attention of the whole class. One interesting way of doing this is to ask the pupils to list what they think they should and should not do in the classroom. This is an exercise which often yields revealing insights to the teacher. Such an exercise is best followed by a discussion of the rules, with some emphasis on why rules are necessary in the classroom, as in everyday life. With younger pupils, it is particularly advantageous if the rules are displayed in a prominent position in the classroom. If the treatment which is going to be applied to a particular pupil is likely to involve ignoring some infractions of the rules, it is important to emphasize that the onus is on the pupils to observe the rules, and that the teacher ought not to have to check the pupils continually to ensure that rules are observed.

At the start of treatment, the teacher must have a clear idea of what changes he would like to see in the pupil's behaviour. Careful judgement is required. It may seem obvious that the pupil who chatters incessantly and does little work ought not to behave in this way. However, it may be that the teacher would find a certain degree of chit-chat to be an essential ingredient in a happy working atmosphere. There is a delicate balance involved. Normal pupils do break rules from time to time, and teachers expect this to happen. Teachers only become concerned when such behaviour is carried to extremes.

When an initial form of treatment proves to be ineffective, the teacher must generate a further treatment strategy. The various available classroom reinforcers must be considered, and perhaps also the introduction of a potentially more powerful, yet artificial, form of reinforcement. At this point, it might well be advisable to discuss the planned treatment with other members of the staff, since it may have implications with which they ought to be acquainted. In one investigation (Wheldall and Austin, 1980), for example, the 'on task' behaviour of a secondary school class was improved by allowing the pupils to earn points which could be traded off for free time during a Friday afternoon lesson. Whilst this kind of strategy can be very successful, other teachers do need to be aware of what is happening. It is not difficult to imagine the reaction of a head-teacher who is unaware that such a strategy is being used, when he calls at the classroom to talk with the teacher. Fortunately, in the example given, the head-teacher was himself the classroom teacher, but even so, had he not kept his colleagues informed, there might have been some strange speculations amongst the staff.

When it becomes impossible for a teacher to devise an effective treatment, advice must be sought. Initially, this may be from other members of the school staff, but should the pupil's difficulties remain intractable, it may be necessary to involve the Schools' Psychological Service, and to call upon the special skills of the educational psychologist. It would of course be advantageous if the educational psychologist could be consulted during all stages, but since there are many teachers and few psychologists, there is seldom such an opportunity.

6 *Fading the Treatment*

When social reinforcement has been employed as the treatment, fading out is usually relatively easy to accomplish, given the power of intermittent reinforcement.

It is, however, at this stage that the teacher can pay the price for using a more artificial form of treatment. Whenever possible this has to be removed, and this is best done by progressively removing elements of the artificial system, so that, for example, a very structured contract can be more loosely formulated. This may seem to be a very difficult task, yet in practice it is often the case that a pupil's improved behaviour is accompanied by an improved understanding of what is being achieved. In the case of Tom, described in Chapter 1, it was relatively simple to remove a complex contract without any deterioration in behaviour, and in the case of Billy, whose log-keeping was initially dependent upon the teacher's signature for good behaviour, the need for the signature rapidly vanished. It really does seem that, provided the pupil understands the need for such a strategy, and provided his behaviour improves, then it is quite likely that he will eventually see no need for special treatment.

7 *The Timing of an Investigation*

An investigation which is carried out fully will require a considerable time for its completion. It should be as continuous as possible, so that periods involving school holidays and examinations should be avoided if this can be achieved. Given that it takes a while to get to know a pupil, and to appreciate his difficulties, the term immediately following the Christmas holidays would seem to be a good time to conduct an investigation, and it does leave the summer term during which to assess the pupil's subsequent performance.

8 *The Design of the Investigation*

No mention of design appeared in the 'guidelines' section of this chapter, since, in order to present an uncomplicated sequence of steps, the section was written as if a simple AB design would be used. However, provided the teacher has the necessary resources for measuring a number of behaviours, and provided baseline observations indicate that behaviours are not interdependent, there is no reason why a multiple baseline design should not be employed.

9 *Treating Academic Behaviours*

The 'guidelines' may seem to have been geared mainly to social forms of behaviour. However, the steps are equally applicable to academic behaviours, when a regular measure can be taken. This was illustrated in the case of Teddy, described in Chapter 1, whose word production was measured daily.

On the other hand, an investigation which requires an initial pre-treatment test, and a final post-treatment test, perhaps using standardized measures (page 55), may not require all the steps outlined, although if possible, some interim measures of progress should be included.

Concluding Comments

It cannot be emphasized too strongly that behaviour modification investigations are undertaken by teachers in their own classrooms. The guidelines offered above should provide a good understanding of the techniques, and of the principles underlying these techniques; but this is no substitute for undertaking one's own investigation. There is abundant evidence that behaviour modification works in classrooms, and provided an investigation is properly conducted, it should work for you in your classroom. It may take a certain amount of thought and effort, but the experience will be invaluable.

Chapter 6

Selected Examples of Behaviour Modification in Schools

Behaviour modification techniques were very seldom used in British schools before 1970, but in the following ten years there was a very rapid development. The initial impetus came from investigations in the USA, and it is probably fair to say that early British investigations (Ward, 1971, 1973; Harrop and Critchley, 1972) were designed to test whether behaviour modification techniques could be applied successfully in this country. When once this stage was passed, the scene was set for the investigation of a variety of educational problems.

The main aim of this chapter is to give the reader an appreciation of the ways in which behaviour modification techniques have been used in schools, with particular emphasis on schools within the British educational system. However, a systematic survey has not been attempted, since it would be impossible to do justice to all the available research within the confines of a single chapter.

As an aid to the reader, who may well be concerned primarily with one particular kind of pupil, the early parts of the chapter are subdivided into research in primary, secondary and special schools, although it must be emphasized at the outset that there is considerable overlap between the techniques used in these three settings.

The Primary School

A large proportion of the early research took place in primary schools because the conditions were less complex than in secondary schools; for example, one teacher was with the class during most or all of the school day. Much of this early work was concerned with the selective use of attention and the application of classroom rules; and whilst this approach is still very much used, as many of the cases detailed in Chapter 1 illustrate, it would be repetitive to include any further such examples in this chapter. Accordingly, the investigations described in this section are illustrative of rather different approaches.

Jack

McNamara (1977) reported a case which embodied some unusual features. Jack, the pupil concerned, was a rather disruptive member of a class of 33 third and fourth year juniors. He was considered to be of average ability, but his work was of a poor standard. During lessons, Jack would continually call out without waiting to be asked to speak, or alternatively he would 'switch off' and play with some physical object, a pencil, ruler, or something brought into school.

During baseline observations the teacher recorded verbal and manipulative interruptions.

(a) Verbal interruptions consisted of 'calling out when given specific instructions to raise hand, and whistling, moaning, or calling to pupils across the class'.

(b) Manipulative interruptions comprised 'playing with small objects, snatching and interfering with other pupils at the same table, tapping feet or other part of the body, lifting the table with knees'.

The baseline lasted for two weeks, and the teacher recorded the number of incidents of each behaviour during the last 15 minutes of each morning session, that is, between 12.00 and 12.15 p.m. each day. For each behaviour, the average number of incidents noted was seven per 15-minute session.

The teacher treated Jack's behaviour by ignoring his verbal and manipulative interruptions, and paying attention to his appropriate behaviours. Jack was given more opportunites for oral work than usual, reporting to the class on a topic, and taking part in a play. The pupils near to him were praised when they showed correct behaviour.

In the one week in which this treatment was applied, Jack's recorded interruptions dropped considerably to averages of three per 15 minutes (verbal) and two per 15 minutes (manipulative). Based on the figures alone, this looked like a successful treatment. However, the data were not considered by the teacher to be an accurate representation of Jack's behaviour, which had deteriorated. He had begun to come into class late, and his manipulative interruptions had become more pronounced. He had, for example, on one occasion, performed a cartwheel in class. This escalation was considered to be Jack's response to the teacher's ignoring of his manipulative interruptions.

A new and more powerful strategy was adopted. Jack was given 20 stars each day. One star was subtracted for any verbal or manipulative interruption. Provided he had not lost more than five stars before 3.00 p.m. in a day, he was allowed to spend the last 30 minutes of the school day on a classroom activity of his own choice. This worked. He regularly gained his 30 minutes activity, and his interruptions decreased markedly. He informed his teacher that he was beginning to enjoy his work, which he had formerly disliked. The teacher found him to be receptive to praise for work well done, and considered that, in time, it might be possible to sustain the improved behaviour without having to rely upon the special treatment.

COMMENT There are several features of this case which need to be considered. The first is by no means unusual, and is yet another example of an initial treatment which was insufficiently powerful to bring about change. A second feature is the way in which the treatment was considered to be unsuccessful. The data extracted were correct, yet misleading. Inappropriate behaviour occurred much less frequently, yet it was more intense. This is not a common response to treatment, but it is a response for which a teacher needs to be continually alert.

The successful treatment had some of the hallmarks of a contract. However, it involved the teacher in looking for inappropriate behaviour rather than for appropriate behaviour, and in view of Jack's reaction to the initial treatment, this would seem to be a very logical approach to take. Whilst the treatment may appear to be negatively focussed, it did lead to a reward, and the treatment was effective. Although the report does not include any long-term information, Jack's inappropriate behaviour was alleviated by the special treatment, and there were hopes that his improvement could be maintained when the treatment was removed.

Ann

Yule, Berger and Wigley (1977) reported the case of a five-year-old girl, Ann, who refused to transfer to the infant school reception class. She had attended a nursery class in the same school on a part-time basis since she was three. Ann's response to joining the reception class took the form of screaming and weeping, so that the issue was not forced. She was sent with a message to the class each day, but she wouldn't stay for more than a couple of minutes. In addition, Ann stayed with her teacher in the staffroom during lunch time, when she should really have been playing in the playground.

It was decided that Ann's difficulties could be considered as three separate problems:

(a) not going to the playground during lunch time;
(b) not being in her proper class in the morning; and
(c) not being in her proper class in the afternoon.

These three problems were treated sequentially.

Initially, lunch time was singled out. Ann was told that 'children were not meant to be in the staffroom and that she could either play in the corridor, or go to the playground with a friend for 15 minutes.' In the words of the investigators, 'To everyone's amazement, Ann went to the playground and stayed during the entire lunch period.' This she continued to do throughout the rest of the investigation (some six weeks).

In the next stage, 'Ann was asked to go to the reception class for ten minutes at some time in the afternoon.' A time was selected when activities which she enjoyed were taking place, and it was arranged that she left whilst she was still happy.

In the third stage, a similar strategy was followed in the mornings.

By the following term, Ann was spending the whole day in the right class, and her continuing progress seemed ensured.

COMMENT This is a nice example, because it touches upon a frequently voiced criticism of behaviour modification, that is, that it is all common sense. And yet, as the investigators pointed out, the teachers had adopted a common sense approach to Ann's difficulties with little success.

A second important feature of this example is the use of the multiple-baseline design. This was a simple, straightforward investigation, and when the pupil's difficulties were analyzed into three distinct components, the design was seen to fit, not only for methodological reasons, but also because a progressive introduction of treatment seemed to be the logical way to proceed.

Two Primary Classes

Tsoi and Yule (1976) reported an investigation in which the behaviour of all the pupils in two primary school classes was treated. In addition, three individual pupils from each class were selected for treatment during specific times in the course of the investigation. The pupils were aged ten to eleven years.

Independent observers were used in this investigation, so that a wide range of behaviours was observed. Five categories of 'off task' behaviour were recorded:

(a) talking to another pupil when not permitted;
(b) inappropriate noise;
(c) inappropriate locality;
(d) aggression;
(e) non-attending.

In addition, two categories of appropriate behaviour were recorded:

(a) appropriate verbal behaviour;
(b) appropriate motor behaviour.

These categories were all carefully defined (Tsoi and Yule 1976, p. 132).

Observations were conducted three or four times per week for sessions of approximately 30 minutes. Interval recording was used, and the observers spent alternately 10 seconds observing and 5 seconds recording. In each 10 seconds of observation, the observers watched only one pupil. This was either one of the selected pupils, or one of the non-selected pupils. A strict rotation was adhered to, the order being: selected pupil 1, non-selected pupil, selected pupil 2, another non-selected pupil, selected pupil 3, another non-selected pupil, and so on. This order continued throughout each observation session. Each of the selected pupils was observed many times, and all of the non-selected pupils were observed in turn.

Baseline observations were taken during ten sessions.

TREATMENT Two conditions of treatment were used. These were group reinforcement contingent upon individual behaviour, and group reinforcement contingent upon group behaviour. The basic difference was that in the former condition all the pupils received the reinforcement when the behaviour of the selected pupils improved, whereas in the latter condition, the total behaviour of the class had to be improved for the reinforcement to be received. The reinforcement, which was selected by the pupils, was five minutes' extra play-time.

In the first condition, one selected pupil was concentrated upon for four or five sessions. A chart of the pupil's 'off task' behaviour was put up in the classroom, and the teacher explained to the pupils just what were considered to be appropriate and inappropriate behaviours, and that the aim was to encourage one pupil to behave well. If the graph showed a drop from one day to the next, or if the level was maintained, the whole class would obtain the extra 5 minutes play-time. After 4 or 5 sessions, a different selected pupil was focussed upon, and so on.

In the second condition, it was explained to all the pupils that a count would be made of the 'off task' behaviour of all the members of the class, so that they were all responsible for obtaining their extra 5 minutes of play-time.

The design of the investigation was relatively complex. The two classes met the two conditions in different orders, as shown below:

CLASS 1	CLASS 2
1 Baseline	1 Baseline
2 Group reinforcement contingent upon individual behaviour	2 Group reinforcement contingent upon group behaviour
3 Return to baseline conditions	3 Return to baseline conditions
4 Group reinforcement contingent upon group behaviour	4 Group reinforcement contingent upon individual behaviour
5 Follow up	5 Follow up

The treatment programme took place during the Spring term, and terminated three weeks before the Easter holidays. The week before and after the holiday were used for the follow up observations. At this stage, the teachers were asked to carry on in whatever way they liked. One continued with group reinforcement contingent upon individual behaviour, the other with group reinforcement contingent upon group behaviour.

RESULTS Both kinds of treatment showed equally effective results with the classes in general. 'Off task' behaviour decreased considerably. However, whilst all the selected pupils improved their behaviour in response to the two conditions, there were marked individual differences between the selected pupils. Most of these pupils improved when the group was reinforced, although one pupil reduced his 'off task' behaviour only when he was the 'named' pupil, whilst the other selected pupils tended to improve even when another pupil was named.

All of the selected pupils, except one, maintained their improved behaviour during the follow-up.

COMMENT The most important feature of this investigation lies in the treatment of whole classes of pupils. As the investigators say, 'class teachers are rightly very quick to point out to the psychologist that they, the teachers, have to deal with whole classes – often as many as thirty in numbers'. The results of this investigation demonstrate that behaviour modification can achieve beneficial results with a whole class.

However, this investigation examined more than whether a whole class, and individual pupils within a class, could be successfully treated. It also compared two different kinds of treatment. This was facilitated by ensuring that each of the two classes met the two kinds of treatment in different orders. The reasoning behind this procedure may not be immediately evident, but when one treatment follows another, it is difficult to see what are the effects of the second treatment, and it becomes impossible to compare the effects of the two kinds of treatment. For example, consider a disruptive pupil who is treated first by reinforcing his own appropriate behaviour, and then by reinforcing the appropriate behaviour of the class. If his behaviour improves markedly under each condition, can one legitimately assume that the outcome would have been the same if the order of treatment had been reversed? The prudent answer must be no. He may have learned to discriminate under the first condition and this may have generalized to the second.

In this investigation, it was demonstrated that in general both the treatment conditions were equally effective. However, the investigators noted that group reinforcement techniques 'maintain the class as a compact component and encourage the children to work toward a common goal', whilst group reinforcement techniques contingent upon individual behaviour 'provide a possible avenue to integrate a disruptive child back to the group if he can take up the responsibility to gain reinforcement for his peers'.

Another interesting feature of this investigation was the selection of the reinforcer for the class. Five minutes extra play-time does not seem to be a particularly large reward, and yet it produced very considerable improvements in the behaviour of the pupils. At the time of the follow up, the total 'off task' behaviour of the pupils in the two classes had been reduced to less than 40 per cent of its original level. For the individual pupils, the 'off task' behaviour was reduced even further, ranging from 13 per cent to 25 per cent of its original level, apart from the one pupil whose improved behaviour was not maintained during the follow up.

Finally, it may be asked, what about the pupil whose improved behaviour was not maintained during the follow up? To be precise, this pupil's behaviour was considerably improved during both treatment conditions, and reverted to its original baseline level during the follow up stage, when the teacher was using group reinforcement contingent upon group behaviour. Just why this was so, we shall never know, although the investigators noted that the pupil had a complex psychiatric background, and that a more continuous individual programme might well be required.

What is evident here is that behaviour modification techniques can be used not only to answer questions such as, 'How can a class teacher deal with a whole class?'; they can also, by means of careful recording, show which pupils are not responding in the same way as their peers.

A Class of Fourth Year Juniors

Merrett and Wheldall (1978) reported an investigation in which the behaviour of an unstreamed class of fourth year junior school pupils was treated. This was a class which was recognized by the headmaster and the staff as containing a high proportion of pupils with behaviour problems. There were 32 pupils in the class.

The pupils were seated around four groups of tables. The teacher had just completed her probationary year, and admitted to some difficulty in gaining and maintaining order in the classroom.

Four kinds of inappropriate pupil behaviour were identified and defined. The names are not all immediately self-explanatory, so they are quoted in full from the report:

(a) Gross motor movement: turning round (more than 90 degrees from the front-facing position), rocking chair, having legs not in contact with the seat of the chair, moving around the room.

(b) Verbalizing: calling out, talking to neighbour (this would include any talking at all if silence had been asked for).

(c) Aggression: touching, striking, hitting, poking, shoving another child with the hand or other object.

(d) Any other behaviour: day-dreaming, gazing around, watching other children.

In addition, appropriate behaviour was identified and defined as:

On task: looking at a study material, reading, writing, cutting, drawing, and so on. This to be marked only when no other category is ticked.

The teacher recorded the behaviour using a time-sampling technique. (Time-sampling has been described on page 63.) Additionally, one of the investigators was present and made recordings as an independent observer during more than half of the observation sessions. The teacher made her recordings whenever she heard a 'ping' from a cassette recorder. This ping was emitted at variable times, but averaged once per minute. When the teacher heard the ping, she would look at a particular, pre-selected pupil, and note the pupil's behaviour by ticking an appropriate column on her record sheet. For successive pings, the behaviour of different pupils was noted.

Baseline observations were taken during nine weeks in the Autumn term.

During the Christmas holiday the teacher read a good deal about behaviour modification techniques, and subsequently had discussions with one of the investigators. It was at this stage that the teacher decided upon the treatment to be employed.

INITIAL TREATMENT Rules were displayed in the classroom. These were:

(a) We stay in our seats whilst working.
(b) We get on quietly with our work.
(c) We try not to interrupt.

Attention was frequently drawn to the rules.

The pupils were given the rules of a game which they were to play with the teacher. Each time the ping was heard, the teacher looked at one of the four tables (this was in a pre-determined, random order, but arranged so that each table was looked at an equal number of times), and if all the pupils were observing the rules, each pupil at the table would receive a house point. This was accompanied by social reinforcement from the teacher.

AMENDED TREATMENT After five weeks of the former treatment, when the pupils' behaviour had been considerably improved, the treatment was faded to 50 per cent of its original level. Points were awarded for only 50 per cent of the pings, and this was determined on a random basis.

RESULTS 1 The behaviour of the pupils improved under both conditions. During the initial treatment, disruptive behaviour dropped to some 36 per cent of its baseline level, and during the amended treatment a further drop to around 27 per cent was noted. At the same time, on-task behaviour increased, so that during the amended treatment the percentage increase of on task behaviour was approximately 100 per cent above the baseline level.

2 A subjective estimate of the classroom indicated a great improvement in orderliness and quiet during classroom work periods. There was an attempt made to measure changes in academic output, and samples of written work were taken during baseline sessions and during one treatment session. From these samples, the investigators noted that the pupils' mean output of written work had increased from 5 words per minute to 13 per minute.

3 The teacher found the recording to be initially 'tedious and

time-consuming', but said it became easier with practice. Having another person in the room she found upsetting, and putting up a chart of rules made her feel silly. On the other hand, she agreed that the game had produced an immediate and very effective change in the pupils' behaviour. She said that she would continue to use behaviour modification techniques.

4 Accuracy checks were made throughout the investigation, and these yielded an average percentage agreement of 88.5 per cent between the recordings of the teacher and of the independent observer.

5 At the end of the investigation, the pupils were asked for their opinions of the 'game'. Except for one girl, they all approved and said that they found the quietness which the game produced, 'enabled them to concentrate and get on with their work without interruption'. The girl who disapproved found the ping to be distracting, but liked the opportunity of earning house points.

COMMENT This investigation is similar to the previous example (Tsoi and Yule, 1976) in two very important respects. It demonstrates once again that the behaviour of a whole class of pupils can be improved by the use of behaviour modification techniques, and it shows that the reinforcement for the pupils, house points, need not be of any great magnitude. Indeed, in this example, it must be emphasized that the reinforcement was a normal school practice, although it must be added that the investigators noted that the house point system had just been introduced, and it, in turn, was backed up by the award of badges to be worn in school. This is a very nice example of the use of rewards in school.

The investigation differed from the previous one in a number of interesting ways. The teacher selected the treatment, and recorded the behaviour; and attention was paid to indicators of success other than the behaviours which were recorded.

Having read about behaviour modification, and after discussions with one of the investigators, the teacher must have felt that this 'game' approach, based on an earlier investigation of Barrish, Saunders and Wolf (1969) in the USA, was most appropriate to her situation. However, in the original investigation, very powerful rewards were used, for example, 30 minutes' free time for the winning team, whilst the losing team had to stay in after school if they had any work not completed. In view of the results obtained by the teacher using house points, the original investigation seems in retrospect, to have departed more than was necessary from normal school practices, although one can never be sure of the conditions which exist within a classroom. It is a great strength of the investigation under discussion that an existing school practice was selected as the means of reinforcement.

In addition to selecting the treatment, the teacher recorded the behaviour. This was one of the primary objectives of the investigation, since if behaviour modification is to be used by teachers with whole classes, the teachers themselves must be able to record the results. To ensure that this objective could be achieved, it was necessary for an independent observer to record at the same time as the teacher. This was done very frequently, during some 60 per cent of the recording session, and the levels of agreement were such that the investigators were confident that the teacher could record the behaviours whilst carrying out her normal teaching role. On the other hand, the teacher's comments do indicate a certain degree of anxiety that the recording was hindering her teaching, particularly in the earlier stages of the investigation. However, against this must be set 'the confidence she gained in controlling the class and the much greater output of work she could expect from them'.

There were other indicators of success in this investigation. All the pupils except one approved of the game, and although the only objective evidence quoted by the investigators concerns a comparison of the average number of written words during baseline sessions with the average number of written words during one treatment session, this is stronger evidence than mere speculation.

It might be felt that the 'ping' was an unnecessary intrusion to the teaching environment. However, in this investigation, the ping was an integral part of the game which was played, so that it was actually a necessary part of the treatment. It should also be remembered that the game received approval from the pupils, with the exception of the girl who found the ping to be distracting.

There is an interesting similarity here with the previously discussed investigation, in which one pupil's behaviour did not improve over the whole course of the investigation. Such results serve to underline that behaviour modification is concerned with individual pupils, and that one can never assume that all pupils will react in the same way to the same conditions. However, too much should not be made of this point in the context of the investigation, and in view of what was achieved. A teacher selected a treatment, using an existing school practice as a reward, recorded the pupils' behaviour, and produced a considerable improvement in the behaviour of an unstreamed class of 32 pupils, many of whom were acknowledged to have behaviour problems.

Pupils with Low Self-concepts

A behaviour modification investigation of a rather different kind from those which have been previously discussed, was undertaken by the writer (Harrop, 1977a). Five primary school teachers, from four different primary schools were involved in the investigation. All four schools were in locations which could be designated as low socio-economic areas.

The investigator administered a questionnaire, the Piers-Harris Self Concept Scale, to the pupils in all five classes, and to four other classes (control classes) drawn from the same schools. This scale had just been standardized, although not reported until later (Chapman, 1981), in the same area in which the investigation was conducted.

The questionnaire required pupils to respond to statements with a yes/no response. Examples of the statements are:

I am a happy person.
I have good ideas.
I give up easily.
I feel left out of things.

When the questionnaires were marked, they yielded scores which indicated how the pupils viewed themselves. The teachers were given the scores of their pupils, together with the booklets containing the pupils' answers. The teachers were asked to select within a week, 'those pupils who they felt had unrealistically low self-concepts, as measured by the questionnaire'.

When the investigator met with each teacher a week later, the selection of pupils was discussed, and each teacher selected either six or seven pupils.

TREATMENT After some discussion, each teacher agreed to carry out the following treatment:

(a) To seek opportunities to reinforce achievements. If achievements were few, to try to find tasks that the pupil could do, and praise whenever possible.
(b) To try to avoid giving the pupil any tasks he could not perform. If failures were to occur, to try and ignore them, or at least be encouraging about attempts.
(c) To try to give the pupil some status within the class, and to try to reinforce other pupils who made positive comments about the pupil.

This treatment programme was carried out by the teachers for four months. After four months, all the classes were retested.

RESULTS An analysis of the results proved to be more complicated than the investigator had anticipated. It had been hoped that the self-concept scores of the pupils selected for treatment would increase considerably, and that the other pupils in the same classes who had not been treated would show minor changes, whilst little change would be seen in the scores of the pupils in the four control classes. The results were not as straightforward as this, and a distinction had to be made between the younger pupils (first two years of the junior school), and the older pupils (final two years of the junior school).

Briefly, the findings were as follows:

(a) For the younger pupils, the average change in the scores of the pupils who were treated showed an increase which was statistically significant, whilst the average change of the scores of the other pupils in the same classes, and the average change in the scores of the pupils in the younger control classes showed no significant change.

(b) For the older pupils, no significant increases were found.

It must be added here, that whilst the results may suggest that the treatment was successful with the younger pupils, the average increase in their scores was comparatively small, that is, approximately 10 per cent. That the results were statistically significant means that they were unlikely to have come about by chance.

COMMENT The inclusion of this investigation in the chapter may seem to be something of a major departure from the normal approach of behaviour modifiers. This is precisely why the investigation was included. The investigation was undertaken because it did seem to the writer that when a pupil's behaviour is treated and improved, there must be a change occurring in the way the pupil views himself.

The investigation was aimed at producing and measuring such a change. That no large changes were seen may be due to the measuring instrument being insufficiently sensitive, or it may be that the treatment was inappropriate.

If the results are accepted as being encouraging with the younger pupils, because of the small increases in the scores of the treated pupils, and discouraging with the older pupils, a possible explanation may be found in the research of Livesley and Bromley (1973). They found the eighth year to be a critical time in the development of person perception. At about this age, a young child's description of people moves from the concrete, appearance, identity, possessions and family, to the more abstract, dispositions, values and beliefs. This being so, it may be that the treatment caught the younger pupils at this critical stage, and that the older pupils had passed through this stage. Or alternatively, the teacher may just be a more reinforcing person to pupils of a younger age group.

It must be admitted that this investigation did not obtain the same kind of success as those which have been previously discussed, and that it was essentially a group comparison study, neglecting the results of individual pupils. However, the investigation does illustrate that behaviour modification need not be confined to physical behaviours in the classroom; and whilst the results are merely indicative, they may well contain useful implications for future research.

The Secondary School

Virginia

Presland (1980) reported a case in which the behaviour of a third year pupil, Virginia, was treated by a teacher, in a class which had been specifically set up to cope with 18 very disruptive pupils. The school was a non-selective secondary school for girls. The teacher was attending a behaviour modification workshop for teachers which met weekly with the investigator.

The teacher was asked to identify which of Virginia's behaviours she would like to change. She selected 'dumb insolence' and 'deliberate non-participation in oral lessons'. The behaviour which she wished to see Virginia adopt more frequently was 'taking part in lessons in a cheerful and cooperative manner'. For systematic observation, the behaviour selected was 'refusing to participate in oral lessons'.

The teacher taught the class for five 35-minute lessons per week, and took baseline observations for two weeks. During this time, she counted the number of times such refusals took place, that is, she used frequency recording.

INITIAL TREATMENT The teacher explained to the class that she would award points to individual pupils for good behaviour, and for work well done. These points could be exchanged for later rewards, but these rewards were not specified. This treatment was put into operation.

SUBSEQUENT TREATMENT After a week, the teacher discussed with the pupils the kind of rewards they would like. It was agreed between the pupils and the teacher that when any pupil reached 30 points, a letter would be sent by the teacher to the pupil's parents, telling them how well the pupil was doing. This treatment continued through a second week.

RESULTS During the baseline observations, Virginia averaged 2.5 refusals to participate per lesson. During the first week of treatment, this dropped to an average of 0.66 refusals to participate, and to zero in the second week.

The teacher reported that there was a marked improvement in Virginia's behaviour in the first week of treatment, and that during the second week she became 'a different girl – cooperative, helpful in and out of the classroom and very happy'. In addition, other teachers commented on Virginia's improved behaviour.

COMMENT This case is a good example of how a secondary school teacher can successfully treat a pupil by using behaviour modification techniques, and perhaps the most important feature of the investigation is that the teacher taught this class for only five 35-minute lessons a week. This is very different from most of the investigations undertaken in primary schools, where the teacher is with the class for large parts of the day.

The treatment which was used, as in many of the other cases, was based on rewarding behaviour which is incompatible with the 'unwanted' behaviour, that is, rewarding good behaviour and work well done, which was incompatible with 'refusing to participate in oral lessons'. In this investigation, the whole class was treated, and in view of the fact that this was a class specifically constituted for disruptive pupils, this seems to have been a very sensible arrangement.

The use of two distinct stages of treatment is interesting, and it seems very likely that during the first stage of treatment the pupils were wondering what the reward would be and perhaps discussing this amongst themselves. If this were so, then the usefulness of the discussions with the teacher on the precise nature of the reward would have been enhanced. That a letter to be sent home to the parents was selected as the reward is not too surprising in view of the results obtained by Burns (1978), which have been discussed in Chapter 3, when he found that girls and boys in secondary schools put 'a favourable report sent home' as top of their list of incentives.

When the results of the investigation are examined, it is seen that the teacher noted a considerable change in the pupil's behaviour. The 'unwanted' behaviour decreased to zero very rapidly, and the pupil became 'a different girl'. Other teachers noted the change. This was achieved in an investigation taking four weeks, and demonstrates how quickly behaviour modification techniques can produce changes in pupils' behaviour.

Billy

MacMillan and Kolvin (1977) reported a case in which an eleven-year-old boy, Billy, was treated by his teacher during the eight lessons per week in which she taught his class. Billy was a disruptive pupil, he would shout out, talk to his neighbours, poke and shove his classmates, and he needed constant prompting and encouragement to attend to his work.

An independent observer made the observations, and recordings of Billy's 'task-relevant' behaviour were taken once a week.

Baseline observations took place during the course of three weeks, and showed Billy's task relevant behaviour to occur approximately 63 per cent of the time.

INITIAL TREATMENT Social reinforcement was selected as the treatment. The teacher paid as much attention as possible to Billy when he behaved appropriately, following the adage 'catch him being good', and used disapproval only when Billy's behaviour could not be tolerated. The practice of prompting Billy to re-start working when he stopped was discontinued.

RESULTS Billy began to improve, and by the sixth week of treatment, he was averaging 80 per cent task-relevant behaviour. At this stage the teacher found him to be much better in class, and reported him to be 'very rarely attention-seeking in a disruptive way now – he is seeking attention through his good behaviour and marks'.

However, in the seventh and eighth weeks, Billy's behaviour and work standards decreased. The teacher noted this, and felt that perhaps she had slackened off in her social reinforcement, or, alternatively, that her attention might have lost its effectiveness for Billy.

SUBSEQUENT TREATMENT To arrest this deterioration in Billy's behaviour, the teacher decided to be more specific in her comments to Billy, 'referring to the fact that Billy was being quiet, working well, and so on.' Once again, his behaviour improved, and levelled out at above 80 per cent task-relevant behaviour. The teacher was very satisfied with this level of behaviour; and at the end of the treatment programme she commented that she was able to find 'plenty of opportunity to praise throughout the lesson'.

COMMENT The first and most obvious reason for considering this investigation is that it does show it to be possible for a teacher to use social reinforcement techniques successfully in a secondary school classroom. And since the investigation only took place during eight lessons per week with the teacher, Billy must have been quite capable of discriminating the 'handling' he was receiving from this particular teacher. The selective use of reinforcement increased his task-relevant behaviour.

At the same time, it cannot be assumed that social reinforcement is likely to succeed with all pupils; indeed, in the same article, the investigators describe the treatment of a pupil for whom social reinforcement was ineffective. He seemed to be 'embarrassed by praise', and was eventually treated by means of a contract.

A second feature of the investigation concerns the deterioration in behaviour which was observed after six weeks of successful treatment. This may only have been a minor perturbation which would have righted itself, but the change was noted rapidly, and the teacher adjusted her treatment accordingly. Had she not altered her treatment, the behaviour might have continued to deteriorate. Her action emphasizes the need for a teacher to scrutinize the data continually, to be alert for such changes as and when they occur, as there is always a danger that a successful treatment may begin to lose its effectiveness.

In practice, teachers who use behaviour modification techniques are continually making minor adjustments in their treatment of pupils. It is easy to decide to give a pupil social reinforcement for working well in class, but it is not so easy to carry out this decision. When this is looked at in terms of specific teacher behaviours, it is a very complex undertaking. Giving attention to a pupil so as to reinforce his behaviour is an extremely 'sensitive' task. Fortunately, teachers do have a very varied repertoire of behaviours upon which they can draw. However, even this varied repertoire does need itself to be varied from time to time, if the pupil is to be reinforced continually by the teacher's attention.

Anthony

McNamara (1979) reported a case in which the behaviour of a second year pupil, Anthony, was treated by the method of self-recording. The teacher concerned with the investigation taught the class twice a week. He selected Anthony for treatment. Anthony was described by the teacher as a 'loner' who was badly behaved in a 'sneaky way'.

The investigator enlisted the aid of two students from a local College of Higher Education to act as observers, so that a comprehensive list of 'unwanted' behaviours was drawn up for recording. The behaviours recorded were:

(a) Calling out answers without raising hand or being asked
(b) Calling out irrelevant comments
(c) Chatting to classmates
(d) Muttering to self (but audible to observers)
(e) Turning away from the teacher when he was talking to the class
(f) Leaving the seat unnecessarily

The observers used interval recording, dividing each recording session into 10 second intervals.

Baseline recordings took place over three weeks, and six observation sessions were completed.

TREATMENT Immediately after the baseline, the teacher talked with Anthony, and discussed his lack of progress in school. He indicated his desire that Anthony should improve, and said he wanted to help. However, before making any decision about what to do, he said that he wanted Anthony to keep a record of his own behaviour, to see whether there really was a problem.

At this point, it was explained to Anthony that he would be given a slip of paper at the start of each lesson, and that he would have to fill in the slip and hand it in at the end of the lesson. On the slip, Anthony had to record the number of times he had talked during the lesson when talking was not required. He had also to sign the slip under the heading, 'This is an honest record of my behaviour.'

When the slips were collected at the end of each lesson, the teacher made no comment about improved behaviour, but did show appreciation for accuracy of recording. This was to try and ensure that it was the self-recording, rather than the teacher's approval which was producing any change in Anthony's behaviour.

This treatment was put into practice for four weeks, and eight observation sessions took place.

RESULTS In the baseline stage of the investigation, the observers' record sheets showed that Anthony behaved inappropriately during an average of 32 per cent of the observation intervals, that is, about once every 30 seconds. In the treatment stage, the records showed that Anthony behaved inappropriately during an average of 1 per cent of the recording intervals, that is, about twice per 35 minute lesson. This was a very dramatic improvement.

It might be thought that the presence of the observers had something to do with Anthony's improvement; however, the investigator was well aware of this possibility. Another badly behaved pupil, Joseph, was included in the investigation as a 'control'. Joseph's behaviour was also continually observed throughout the baseline and treatment stages of the investigation, but Joseph was not required to self-record. His behaviour was not treated in any way. Joseph's inappropriate behaviour showed little change throughout the investigation, averaging 21 per cent during the baseline and 17 per cent during the treatment of Anthony. Had the observers' presence been responsible for the improvement in Anthony's behaviour, there would almost certainly have been a similar effect seen in Joseph's behaviour.

Raymond

In the same article, McNamara (1979) reported on two other cases in which the same treatment was used. One of these cases yielded results which were very similar to those obtained with Anthony, but the other case yielded rather disappointing results. Since it is comparatively rare to find a published report which produces inconclusive results, and since such cases may indicate possible pit-falls for the investigator, this latter case is examined in some detail.

Raymond was a first year pupil who was described as being below average in ability and badly adjusted to the classroom. He was selected for treatment by the school year-tutor. The teacher concerned with the investigation taught the class four times a week.

Recordings were taken by two independent observers, and the baseline lasted for one week. However, unlike the previous investigation, the teacher informed the pupil, before the baseline, that he would be observed.

TREATMENT The initial part of the treatment did not differ from the treatment of Anthony. However, when Raymond handed in his recording slips at the end of each lesson, no comment was made to him. The treatment lasted for three weeks.

RESULTS There was a small improvement in Raymond's behaviour, that is, his recorded inappropriate behaviour dropped from 33 per cent of the observation intervals during the baseline to

24 per cent during treatment. The behaviour of another pupil who was also observed throughout the investigation, but was not treated, remained virtually unchanged.

COMMENT In these two examples, we can see that self-recording was very successful with one pupil, yet it was only marginally successful with the other. It is not easy to pin-point exactly why this occurred, but certain clues are evident in the two reports, and three important differences are evident in the ways in which the two investigations were carried out:

(a) It was Anthony's teacher who selected Anthony for treatment, whereas it was the year-tutor who selected Raymond for treatment.
(b) Anthony was not informed before the baseline that he was to be observed, whereas Raymond was informed before the baseline.
(c) When Anthony handed in his recording slips, the teacher commented on his accuracy. This was not done with Raymond.

It is impossible to ascertain the precise effect of these three differences, but it would seem evident that it is better if the teacher selects who is to be treated, and it is easy to see how a teacher's commitment can be decreased when this is not done. Informing Raymond that he was to be observed before the baseline recordings were made might also have had an effect, since he may well have changed his behaviour as a consequence of knowing he was being observed. This may well have had an effect on Raymond's behaviour, although, whilst Anthony was not informed before the baseline that he was being observed, he may well have guessed that he was being watched.

Perhaps the most important difference between the two investigations lies in the way in which the teachers dealt with the pupils' recording slips. Anthony must have been made aware by the teacher's comments that a check was being made on his accuracy. Raymond, on the other hand, did not have the accuracy check brought to his attention. In these circumstances, it seems to be a reasonable assumption that Anthony would take the self-recording task more seriously than would Raymond.

It is perhaps inadvisable to generalize too widely from two investigations, but it does seem evident that self-recording can be a successful form of treatment, when careful attention is paid to the method used. Provided the teacher is concerned about the pupil's difficulties, and shows this concern by discussion and by commenting on the accuracy of the pupil's recording, and provided the pupil appreciates this concern, and sees evidence in the form of accuracy checks being made, then there would seem to be a good chance that self-recording can be a useful technique for the behaviour modifier to employ.

A Class of Fourth Year Pupils

Wheldall and Austin (1980) reported an investigation in which the behaviour of a whole class of fourth year pupils in a comprehensive school was treated. The class consisted of 25 boys and girls, who were below average academically, but who were not the least able pupils in the school.

The investigators began by asking the head teacher to consult with his staff, and locate a particularly 'disruptive' class, that is, the kind of class which evoked feelings of 'not that lot again', and 'thank goodness that's over for another week'. When a class had been selected, the next step was to obtain a volunteer to work with the investigators in attempting to modify the behaviour of the pupils in the classroom. Perhaps not surprisingly, not one of the teachers volunteered. However, the head master took the class for mathematics, and 'in an act of charity', volunteered himself as a subject. Although, not personally encountering what he considered to be major 'disruptive problems', he agreed that the pupils were 'buoyant' and 'inattentive' and that they 'could be troublesome'.

The investigators watched the head master with the class for several lessons, and found his description of the pupils' behaviour to be accurate. Whilst he was a very skilled teacher who had an excellent working relationship with his pupils, there was a good deal of 'off-task' behaviour demonstrated in the classroom, for example, talking, shouting, teasing, playful poking and kicking, tapping pens and desk lids.

Baseline recordings were made during eleven 40-minute mathematics lessons. The observers sat in with the class during the lessons, and recorded the pupils' behaviour. In each recording session, the 25 pupils were observed in turn for 30-second time-intervals. During each 30-second time interval, the time the pupil spent 'on task' was recorded by means of a cumulative timer-stopwatch.

The recordings showed that the average percentage of time the pupils were 'on task' was 55 per cent during the eleven baseline observations.

TREATMENT 1 The investigators had noticed that a large proportion of the 'off-task' behaviour took place when some of the quicker pupils had finished the set task. Since the set task was usually a few problems written on the blackboard, it was decided that the head master should put a few extra problems on the board. This was put into practice for seven lessons, and average 'on-task' behaviour rose from 55 per cent to a fairly stable average of 69 per cent.

TREATMENT 2 It was decided that on-task behaviour needed further improvement. At this point the investigators differed. One investigator was in favour of a 'rules, praise and ignore' strategy, and the other favoured a 'game' strategy. As a compromise, both strategies were included in the treatment, and were used on alternate days.

A RULES, PRAISE AND IGNORE Following discussions with the head master, four basic rules were agreed upon which defined appropriate on-task behaviour. These were:

1 When the teacher is talking to us we look at him.
2 We get on with our work quietly.
3 We try not to stop others from working.
4 We try to pay attention to our work and try not to daydream.

The head master read out these rules at the beginning of every lesson, and from time to time they were referred to during lessons, but not when rule breaking occurred. At the same time, the head praised the pupils, either individually or as a group, when the rules were being observed. Infringements of the rules were ignored, 'unless serious or dangerous disruptions occurred'.

B THE GAME A cassette was prepared which gave an audible chime at variable intervals, but averaging once every two minutes. Whenever a chime was emitted, the head looked to see if all the pupils were observing the rules. If all the pupils were observing the rules, a point was awarded to the class, and praise was given. Each point was worth one minute of free time during the Friday afternoon mathematics lesson; this being a lesson which was often interrupted for various school activities. A score of 25 points meant the whole lesson was a 'free period' for the pupils, and they could talk or play games such as draughts or cards.

RESULTS Initially, on the 'rules, praise and ignore' days, the on-task behaviour rose to over 80 per cent, and on the 'game' days, on-task behaviour rose to over 90 per cent. After 12 lessons, the rates for both conditions reached about 95 per cent.

In addition to this large increase in on-task behaviour, there were other indications of success. Three pupils asked for extra help during their free time, and once, when owing to an oversight the class was left without a teacher, the head found the pupils quietly working on their own. One pupil had devised a quiz which the others were tackling. Needless to say, the head master was impressed with the success of the investigation, and was eager that one of the investigators hold a seminar with the school staff on 'behavioural classroom management'.

COMMENT This investigation has many interesting features, and these will be discussed in the order in which they appeared.

1 The fact that not one teacher volunteered to work with the investigators is not really surprising, since it would have meant inviting the investigators into the classroom. This is a situation which can provoke anxiety even when a 'good' class is being taught, and when a difficult class is being taught a teacher can feel particularly vulnerable. At the same time, the presence of student teachers as observers may produce little anxiety, since they are in the classroom to learn. However, the presence of specialists in behavioural management, may seem, to say the least, rather a threatening situation.

2 Although the head master didn't feel that the class was disruptive, the pupils really did appear to spend a lot of time not working. 55 per cent on-task behaviour during the baseline leaves a good deal of time for other behaviours to occur.

3 Merely putting extra sums on the blackboard for the quicker pupils to work at towards the end of the lesson produced an increase in on-task behaviour. This seems to be a very simple strategy, yet upon examination it does raise an additional issue. It is sometimes felt by teachers that completing set work before the end of a lesson can be rewarding to a pupil, and it could well be argued that this provides the pupil with free time which he has earned. This is indeed a reasonable argument when applied to the quicker pupils. However, when pupils gain free time whilst others are working, it may well be that the free time is put to a use which interferes with the work of the other pupils; and it seems likely that this process was operating in the classroom. Consequently, putting extra problems on the board increased overall 'on-task' behaviour.

4 The two later treatments which were used, 'rules, praise and ignore', alternating with the 'game', produced very large increases in on-task behaviour. One might have expected that the 'game', which could produce a free lesson as reward, would have acted as a more powerful reinforcer than would the use of social reinforcement. This occurred in the short term, but not in the long term.

To be quite fair about this, the head master was the teacher concerned, and as such he may have had more reinforcing properties for the pupils than would some of the other teachers. However, the results of the investigation do indicate, as the investigators say, that 'significant improvements in on-task behaviour may be achieved using only light behavioural technology such as the manipulation of setting events (more sums) or simple rules, praise and ignoring strategies'.

Following the same line of reasoning, it becomes evident that setting up a complex strategy, such as the 'game' used in this investigation, when a strategy which is closer to natural classroom conditions might have been equally effective, is rather an inefficient way of modifying pupils' behaviour. If such a complex strategy proves to be effective, the teacher has then to consider how to fade out the treatment, and runs the risk of losing the gains which have been made.

5 Finally, it must be emphasized that this was a class of fourth year pupils in a comprehensive school. The whole class was treated, and the behaviour of the pupils was considerably improved.

The Special School

Behaviour modification techniques are used far more frequently in special schools than in ordinary schools, and such is the diversity of the work in these schools, that it cannot be adequately sampled in a short section. However, in order that teachers can gain some insight into what is being done, a brief account of the operation of two special schools is included here.

Carr Hall

Carr Hall was a primary day centre for 24 maladjusted pupils aged five to eleven years. The pupils were placed there on the recommendation of the educational psychologist, no attempt was made to ensure a balanced intake, and no pupil was deemed unsuitable for Carr Hall. The centre was in operation for ten terms, until, in 1977, it changed its status to that of a school and moved to new premises. At that point, the senior educational psychologist who worked with the centre staff and the head teacher decided that it was appropriate to report on what had been achieved during the ten terms of operation (McNamara and Moore, 1978). What follows is a summary of that report.

Most of the pupils arriving at the centre were aggressive and disruptive, and consequently would have been difficult to control in an ordinary school. Very few were withdrawn, and very few had the dual handicap of maladjustment coupled with specific learning difficulties. Some of the pupils had been excluded from their previous schools because they were a danger to other pupils.

When they arrived at the centre, most of the pupils were very active and highly distractable.

The aim of the centre was to facilitate the return of the pupils as soon as possible to their normal schools. Specifically, this meant:

(a) establishing good work habits;
(b) removing behaviour which would meet with disapproval in an ordinary school.

In behavioural terms, this usually meant that the pupil ought to be able to work quietly at a set task for 30 minutes without close supervision, and without resorting to behaviours which would cause severe teacher disapproval.

THE CURRICULUM The teachers made extensive use of material which was already organized. These included programmes such as the Sullivan Reading programme, the Distar Reading and Arithmetic programme. Such programmes were selected because they aided the pupils in experiencing measurable progress, and they lifted the burden of curriculum choice from the teachers, enabling them to concentrate on how to teach, and giving opportunities for attention to be paid to individual pupils when learning was taking place.

RULES Each room used by the pupils had its own specific rules, often pinned to the wall, so that appropriate behaviour varied from room to room. In the common room, for example, which was used by staff and pupils, running and shouting was not permitted, whilst in the reading room, which had individual study booths, no talking was allowed between pupils, and the teacher's attention had to be obtained by raising a hand.

THE TIME-TABLE The mornings were always the same each day. This pattern was adhered to so that the pupils would know what was expected of them at any time, and to avoid the possibility of time-wasting which could occur when sequences changed.

TOKENS During the mornings, the pupils received tokens for good work, and for behaviour acceptable at their own level. The giving of tokens was always accompanied by teacher attention. If a pupil accumulated 40 tokens, he could buy a 40-minute option lesson in the afternoon, the options including woodwork, puppet and soft toy making, painting, fishing, kite making and flying, model making, recreation (free time), and so forth. The specific programme for each pupil was designed so that he could 'afford' to purchase an option daily, and a double option about once a week.

Should a pupil not earn sufficient tokens to buy an option, he would attend a compulsory lesson, the topic of which was left to the teacher's discretion. These lessons tended to be aimed at improving basic educational skills.

INDIVIDUAL PROGRAMMES When a pupil was first admitted to the Centre, his teacher decided upon a reward schedule for his behaviour. Shaping played a prominent role throughout a pupil's treatment. If, for example, the pupil's report from his previous school drew attention to a 'short concentration span' or to 'the production of very little work', one of the teacher's first objectives would have been to raise work output. Initially, the pupil might have received one token for 10 written words, and this might have been gradually increased to one token for 50 words. In addition, a 'bonus' would have been built into the arrangement, for 'output' above the agreed level.

When once a pupil adjusted to the system, and as his work output progressively increased, a sequence of negotiations and 'contracts' was set up. The pupil and teacher would agree on the required work output, the award of tokens and the bonus; and, contrary to what one might expect, the pupils were normally over-ambitious about the quantity of work they thought they could produce, and very often the teachers had to persuade the pupils to reduce their estimates.

Careful records were kept of each pupil's progress, so that results could be continually evaluated.

OTHER STRATEGIES

1 *Fines* A token could be deducted for unacceptable behaviour.
2 *Time-Out* Whenever a pupil's behaviour began to escalate towards a level which would render learning impossible for the other pupils, he was required to leave the classroom and went to a withdrawal room. He was allowed to return when he wished. If he had a 'tantrum' in the withdrawal room, he was allowed to return to the classroom half a minute after he had 'settled

down'. The withdrawal rooms were not designed to be frightening; they were ordinary large rooms with windows.

RELATIONSHIPS Great stress was placed upon friendly and informal relationships between staff and pupils. Everyone shared the same common room, and a daily meeting was held in the centre when pupils brought up grievances about one another, about the staff or about the system.

COMMENT In this admittedly brief and selective summary of the report, it can be seen that the staff of Carr Hall employed a very structured use of behaviour modification techniques. The aims were clear, and the treatment of each individual pupil was properly geared towards meeting the aims.

Whilst many of the practices used at Carr Hall have already been discussed in Chapter 2, the authors of the report do make a number of telling comments which are well worth emphasizing. The first concerns the giving of tokens – it will be recalled that the pupils had to receive 40 such tokens during the morning in order to buy an optional lesson. These tokens were always given singly, and with teacher attention, so that in practice, a pupil would receive attention from the teacher up to 40 times during a morning session. This might well have been more attention than he had received for appropriate work in his previous school throughout a whole school term.

A second comment concerns the use of fines. Whilst these were used as punishment, their purpose was to pin-point unacceptable behaviours, and in many cases, this was behaviour which the pupil was unaware that he was doing, for example, day-dreaming, swearing, spitting. Consequently, fining a pupil was aimed at enabling him to discriminate inappropriate behaviour from appropriate behaviour.

A third comment relates to the 'time-out' room. This was used in a preventative way, that is, the teacher was preventing behaviour from escalating to a level which would cause a major disruption in the classroom. The pupil was being removed from a situation in which he could earn tokens, and he could return when he was ready to behave appropriately.

Chelfam Mill

Burland (1979) described the procedures used in Chelfam Mill school, which is a residential school for emotionally disturbed pupils. There are marked similarities between the procedures described at Chelfam Mill and those reported as having been used at Carr Hall, for example, the use of tokens, contracts, fines, time out, the careful keeping of records, and a stress on friendly, informal relationships between pupils and staff. However, the description of Chelfam Mill is more detailed than the report on Carr Hall, and includes a number of valuable additional features.

When a pupil is first introduced to the token system, it is pointed out that younger, or less able pupils have to learn how the system operates, and thus receive small rewards, such as sweets, immediately following appropriate behaviour. Tokens are then introduced gradually.

The tokens may be traded in for a wide variety of goods. There is a token shop, complete with displays and prices, and tokens may be traded in for sweets, cakes, plastic toys, extra T.V., cookery sessions, disco admission, and even breakfast in bed. 'Costs' are adjusted in terms of supply and demand.

As well as individual programmes with pupils, there are also group, class and community programmes. As an example of a group programme, the case of Daniel is quoted.

'Daniel obtained most of his rewarding experiences from disturbing other boys or getting them to laugh at his antics. To control this his peers were rewarded for ignoring Daniel's inappropriate behaviour. They were successful at doing this, but realizing that Daniel could reduce their earning by being well-behaved, and that this situation could actually encourage Daniel's peers to incite him to behave inappropriately, so that they could have the chance to ignore him, it was arranged that the group also earned if Daniel behaved well. This system effectively controlled the inappropriate behaviour.'

The parents of the pupils are also encouraged to become involved in treatment. At an initial interview, the techniques which are used in the school are described, and cooperation is emphasized. Those parents who live fairly close to the school are invited to attend parents' meetings, and training is given. Other parents visit for days or week-ends, and observe the techniques in operation.

COMMENT These two accounts illustrate very extensive uses of behaviour modification practices. Both environments are very structured and consistent in their use of the techniques. Both operate a token economy, and utilize a variety of powerful procedures. The teacher in an ordinary school, and in many special schools, will see Carr Hall and Chelfam Mill as very different from his normal experience, as indeed they are. But it must be remembered that these are differences of practice, rather than of principle.

The principle that the pupil behaves in a way for which he is reinforced holds good in any situation. However, as has been repeatedly emphasized, when normally available classroom reinforcers prove to be ineffective, more powerful techniques must be used. It has also been stressed that if a pupil does not belong in a classroom, then he must be treated in the classroom to which he belongs. This is why the pupils were sent to Carr Hall and Chelfam Mill. Such pupils were not amenable to normally available classroom reinforcers, so that more powerful techniques had to be used; and this section will perhaps have served to illustrate how those techniques have been applied.

General Comments

The examples of the use of behaviour modification in British schools which have been presented in this chapter should serve to illustrate the diversity of the approaches which have been taken by different investigators in different situations. There are, however, many other examples which have not been included, and a useful summary of many of these may be found in an article by Merrett (1981). It must also be added that, in summarizing the various reports which have been discussed, the writer has had to be selective so that features of particular interest and relevance could be presented; in consequence, much material of specialist and scholarly significance has had to be omitted.

Research in other School Systems

Whilst the investigations conducted in the British school system reflect the increasing use of behaviour modification procedures and involve a variety of approaches, there is still much to be learned from a brief examination of some of the applications of behaviour modification in other school systems, particularly work from the USA. There are three main aspects of this research which would seem to be of particular interest. These are the use of modelling, modifying academic performance, and the use of self-management.

Modelling

In one of the earlier investigations, Lovaas, Berberich, Perloff, and Shaeffer (1966) used modelling to help mute schizophrenic children to learn to talk. The model, who was a speech therapist, would make a sound, and when the child made an adequate imitation, reinforcement would be given. By a process of gradual shaping, combined with modelling, the foundations of language were established.

O'Connor (1969) treated pre-school children who had histories of isolate behaviour by letting them watch a film which showed pre-school children playing together and being reinforced for their social activities. The children responded to the film with an increase in their own social behaviour. This increase, according to the children's teacher, was maintained throughout the school year.

Friedrich and Stein (1973) showed nursery school children cartoons depicting aggression, sociable films, and neutral films. Viewing took place daily for nine weeks, and the pupils' behaviour was observed in the classroom. Broadly speaking the behaviour of the pupils mirrored the kind of material which they viewed, for example, those children who viewed the aggressive cartoons showed an increase in rule breaking, whilst those who viewed the sociable films showed more persistence in their appropriate classroom behaviour.

There are not very many reports of investigations conducted with older pupils, and yet it will be recalled that the successful treatment of Tom and Billy (Chapter 1) did produce improved behaviour from the other pupils, and that imitation (modelling) was put forward as a possible explanation. The following investigation shows how such a process may be facilitated.

West and Axelrod (1975) treated three different classes of emotionally disturbed adolescent pupils by allowing them to earn small sums of money for reducing their disruptive behaviour. In two of the classes, very marked reductions in disruptive behaviour were obtained. In the third class, the procedure was rejected as childish, and substantial increases in inappropriate behaviour occurred. The pupils were led by George, a large thirteen-year-old.

A conversation with George indicated that he wished to be given more responsibility, and he agreed to help the investigators by becoming a classroom 'consultant'. His behaviour improved immediately, and following on from this, so did the behaviour of the other pupils, even though no 'reward' was given to the pupils. George, it seems, had been selected as a model for imitation.

It seems evident from these investigations that modelling is a very pervasive influence in the classroom, and its potential influence ought always to be borne in mind when investigations are undertaken. Pupils will imitate, and the models they select can have a critical influence on their classroom behaviours.

Academic Performance

In recent years, there has been a considerable increase in the number of investigations aimed at increasing academic performance. The reported work has an extensive range along many dimensions, so that no attempt is made here to give an overview of what has been investigated.

The aim of this section is to give the reader some appreciation of the kind of investigations which have been undertaken, and, with this end in view, three reports are summarized.

Increasing the Rate of Composition Writing

Van Houten and McKillop (1977) reported an investigation with two classes of pupils aged 15 and 16. The classes were taught English by the same teacher.

Before the investigation began, the teacher listed 50 composition topics which she considered to be of equal difficulty; these were put into a random order, and each topic was assigned to one day of the investigation. Writing a composition each day was planned into the time-table for each class.

BASELINE I At the start of every lesson, each pupil wrote his name on the top of his paper, the teacher wrote the topic on the blackboard, and the pupils were asked to write as much as they could on the topic. Whilst the pupils wrote, the teacher remained at her desk, and gave no praise for writing. When five minutes had elapsed, the pupils were told to stop writing, the papers were collected, and the lesson continued with another activity.

After the school day, the teacher counted the number of words in each composition, but excluded non-sentences and very repetitive sentences. A non-sentence was defined as an incomplete thought, and a repetitive sentence was a sentence which immediately followed another in which all the words were the same, except one.

The baseline continued for five school days.

TREATMENT I On the first day of treatment, the pupils were shown a chart which displayed the maximum number of words each pupil had written on any composition during the previous five lessons. Their attention was drawn to the five-minute timing, and they were asked to try and beat their previous highest score in the five minute period.

At the end of five minutes, the pupils were asked to put down their pens, and to pick up red marking pens. They were instructed to count the words, and enter the total on top of the page.

On the following day, and on each successive day of this treatment phase, which lasted for six days, the scores on the chart were altered whenever a pupil's score exceeded his previous highest score (according to the teacher's scoring).

BASELINE 2 At the start of this phase, the teacher told the pupils that compositions would no longer be timed, but that they must continue to write as much as possible, whilst avoiding incomplete and repetitive sentences. The chart was taken away, and pupils were told that they would no longer be counting their words. Compositions were collected in a casual manner, so that the pupils might not realize they were being timed.

This phase lasted five days.

TREATMENT 2 This phase was the same as the earlier treatment phase, that is, timing was emphasized, the pupils scored their compositions, and the chart was reintroduced.

This phase lasted a further five days.

THE MEASUREMENTS WHICH WERE MADE

1. To check the accuracy of the teacher's scoring, a random sample of the essays, that is, the work done on two of the days from each phase, was independently checked by observers who did not know the purpose of the investigation. Observer agreement averaged 99 per cent.
2. To examine the quality of the compositions, two senior English teachers were given randomly selected pairs of essays from each pupil. Their task was to judge which was the better from each pair, using their own criteria. Each of the teachers received the same pairs of compositions. Their percentage agreement averaged above 80 per cent for the compositions drawn from the two classes of pupils.
3. Finally, in order to ensure that composition length was not used as a cue to evaluating the essays, each of the two teachers was given a portion of each pair of compositions, that is, from the fifteenth to the fiftieth word, and asked to decide which was the better of each pair. It was found that the two judges rated the compositions in the same way, whether they read the whole composition, or just the selected portion, that is, for judge A

this occured for 100 per cent of the compositions, and for judge B, for 98 per cent.

RESULTS

1 *Word Production* The average number of words produced per minute in the two classes was as follows:

Baseline 1	13, 17,	Treatment 1	22, 25,
Baseline 2	15, 20,	Treatment 2	21, 25,

2 *Quality* The independent judges found the compositions written during the treatment phases to be superior to those written during the baseline phases for 80 per cent and 88 per cent of the pairs of compositions.

DISCUSSION The investigators noted that the procedures used had increased the rate of composition writing from senior high school students. Further, the increased writing rate was correlated with increased ratings of story quality by independent judges. However, the investigators were careful to point out that this finding does not mean the same procedures will always produce similar results with other pupils in other situations.

COMMENT This investigation used timing, public posting of individual performance, and self-scoring to increase pupils' academic output both quantitatively and qualitatively. There have been many such investigations with similar results, but prior to the work of Van Houten and McKillop, the focus of attention had been on pupils in the primary school age range.

Whilst, as the investigators point out, it is perhaps unwise to generalize too widely from a single, limited investigation, this research does indicate a potentially fruitful way of increasing the academic performance of whole classes of pupils. It must be added however, that writing a composition in five minutes does seem to be a somewhat unusual procedure, and it would be imprudent to assume that the treatment had resulted in improved composition writing.

The investigation also demonstrates a different way of examining observer agreement, and should serve to illustrate the care which needs to be taken to ensure that the scoring of written responses is conducted as carefully as possible.

Increasing Ability to Write Creatively

Campbell and Willis (1978) reported an investigation with a class of pupils between the ages of ten and twelve. The aim of the investigation was to increase the pupils' ability in writing 'Creative English'.

The investigators based their work on three of the four components considered by Torrance (1962) to be the main components of creative thinking – fluency, flexibility and elaboration. The fourth component, orginality, was not used because it did not lend itself to systematic measurement.

The three components were defined by the investigators as follows:

1 Fluency: the number of different but relevant responses or ideas given to a topic. This form of response can usually be considered in terms of the number of sentences. In the scoring system used, one point was given for each expressed idea relevant to the topic.
2 Flexibility: the change in perspective of thought or particular pattern set from the previous idea or response (sentence). One point was given for each change. Fluency can probably best be differentiated from flexibility by an example. Suppose a student is asked to describe the uses he can make of a tin can, and he replies 'I can put my pencil in it, I can keep water in it, and I can put stones in it and use it to make noise.' He would receive three points for fluency because each of the three responses is different but relevant. However, only two points would be awarded for flexibility because the first two sentences express the same perspective, the use of the can as a container.
3 Elaboration: this involves the degree of response elaboration or 'spelling out' of a particular response or idea given, the amount of information above and beyond what is necessary in communicating the basic idea. Indicators of this were the use of prepositional phrases, conjunctions, adjectives, adverbs, compound sentences, and so forth. A maximum of two points per sentence was given dependent upon the degree of elaboration.

In addition to these detailed definitions, the investigators included an Appendix containing a scoring guide.

As one method of testing the effects of the treatment which was used, a standardized test of creative thinking – the *Torrance Test of Creative Thinking* (1966) – was administered before and after the treatment programme. Alternative forms were used to avoid any carry-over effect from initial to final testing.

THE REINFORCEMENT During treatment phases, pupils were awarded tokens up to a maximum of five, dependent upon work output, and scores were paired with differential levels of teacher approval, so that, for example, five tokens received a comment such as 'that was very, very good', whilst one or two tokens received no comment.

The pay-off for the tokens was a party for the pupils. Music was provided and 'edibles' could be purchased with the tokens.

THE ACADEMIC TASK Before the programme began, the teacher devised 50 topics in the form of 'just suppose' essay titles, which the pupils were to write about for 15 minutes; for example, Just suppose clouds came down from the sky and floated on the ground, Just suppose we could change our faces.

The 50 topics were randomized and each was assigned to a particular lesson during the investigation.

BASELINE At the beginning of the writing session, the teacher explained that the pupils were to write creatively, and that they were not to be concerned with grammar and spelling. Fluency, flexibility and elaboration were described, and the teacher illustrated how pupils could increase their output of each of the three components.

The topic was introduced, and the pupils wrote for 15 minutes. This procedure was in operation for ten days.

TREATMENT I (ELABORATION) At the start of each writing session, the teacher told the pupils that they would receive tokens for elaboration. Tokens, up to a maximum of five, were awarded to each pupil, based on the teacher's scoring for elaboration, and the awarding of tokens was paired with the appropriate level of teacher approval. How many tokens each pupil obtained depended upon a combination of his increases in output from session to session and upon the absolute level of his scores compared with the other pupils.

This procedure continued for nine days, until the pupils' elaboration scores had increased to a fairly stable level.

TREATMENT 2 (ELABORATION AND FLEXIBILITY) At the start of each writing session, the pupils were informed by the teacher that they would receive tokens for elaboration and flexibility. Again tokens were awarded, paired with social reinforcement. The maximum number of tokens given remained at five, but this time the number awarded was determined by a formula which took into account both elaboration and flexibility.

This procedure continued for six days, when an increase in the pupils' scores for elaboration and flexibility was noted.

TREATMENT 3 (ELABORATION, FLEXIBILITY AND FLUENCY) In this phase, the same procedure was followed, except that fluency was included in the treatment.

The phase continued for seven days.

FADE-OUT On the first four days of this phase, tokens and social approval were given for only two essays, which were randomly chosen. For the next four days, only one randomly selected essay was chosen, and for a final four days, tokens and social approval were not given.

THE MEASUREMENTS WHICH WERE MADE To check the teacher's accuracy, an independent judge, who was not aware of the purpose of the investigation, scored 176 essays selected at random, using the same criteria as the teacher. Percentage agreement averaged 87 per cent for elaboration, 90 per cent for flexibility, and 95 per cent for fluency.

RESULTS

1 A multiple-baseline design was used in the investigation. During the baseline phase, the three components of creative writing remained relatively stable. When elaboration alone was treated, elaboration scores increased, whilst scores on flexibility and fluency remained stable. When flexibility, and subsequently fluency were added, the scores on these components increased. During fade-out, elaboration and fluency scores remained relatively high, while fluency decreased, although all the component scores remained well above their baseline levels.
2 On the standardized test of creative thinking, very considerable gains were made by the pupils. The test measured fluency, flexibility and originality, and showed average gains of 53 per cent, 71 per cent, and 44 per cent respectively.
3 At a subjective level, the teacher reported that the pupils really enjoyed the procedure, and it continued to be used after the investigation had concluded. In addition, several other teachers in the school adopted the procedure because of its 'enthusiastic acceptance' by the pupils.

DISCUSSION The investigators noted that their results strongly suggest that procedures based on reinforcement techniques can facilitate creative writing, both in terms of objectively measured components of creativity, and in terms of performance on a standardised test of creative thinking.

COMMENT Creative behaviour is by its very nature difficult to investigate, and whilst there have been a number of published articles which suggest that creative behaviour has been modified, it is not usually difficult to see the flaws in such investigations (Harrop, 1978b). However, creativity is a very challenging area to the behaviour modifier, because so much of the behaviour modification research which has been conducted seems to emphasize a rather narrow view of education, that is, that pupils should not disrupt learning, that pupils should make academic progress, and so forth – not that these are unworthy goals in their own right, of course. On the other hand, the behaviour modifier ought not to remain narrowly focussed, and should surely be alert to the possibility of improving other aspects of pupils' functioning.

In the investigation of Campbell and Willis, there does seem to be good evidence that the awarding of tokens for specific components of creativity can increase creative behaviour as defined by the investigators, although to be academically rigorous, their use of the multiple-baseline design needs to be questioned, since a close scrutiny of their graphs suggests 'fluency' and 'flexibility' are not independent measures. Whilst the procedures used may seem to be a little complex to follow, they are relatively easy to put into practice. The fact that the teacher reported the pupils as enjoying the procedure may mean that the 'party' given to the pupils as a pay-off for tokens is not an essential feature of the investigation, and indeed preliminary research by the writer indicates this to be a reasonable assumption.

Perhaps the most important feature of this investigation lies in the translation of an apparently amorphous term, 'creativity', into behaviours which can be measured with a high level of observer agreement. When such behaviours can be defined, they can be subjected to treatment, and most importantly, treatment can be evaluated.

Increasing Spelling Accuracy

Dineen, Clark, and Risley (1977) reported an investigation with three pupils aged nine and ten who were members of a class of pupils of average intelligence, but with a reading deficiency of two years.

At the start of the investigation, spelling words which were appropriate to the reading age of the pupils were selected, and ordered into six lists of 15 words each.

TUTOR TRAINING Each of the three pupils had a 20 to 30 minute session with the teacher, in which the teacher taught the pupil how to behave both as spelling tutor and as tutee. The teacher used a combination of modelling, shaping and selective reinforcement to achieve this.

WORD IDENTIFICATION Each pupil was taught to identify the words on three of the lists.

SPELLING PRE-TEST Immediately after learning to identify the words, each pupil was given a spelling test in which all the words on the three lists were presented in random order.

TUTORING During normal spelling lessons, which took place twice a day, for 20 minutes, the pupils acted as spelling tutor or tutee for one another using the three lists, that is, Jane taught Norman list 1, Norman taught Brady list 2, and Brady taught Jane list 3.

SPELLING POST-TEST The day following the last tutorial session, each pupil was again given a spelling test which contained the 45 words from the three lists.

THE SEQUENCE REPEATED The experimental sequence had to be repeated with the three other spelling lists, because whilst Jane had taught Norman, Norman had taught Brady, and Brady had taught Jane, the reverse was not true, that is, Norman had not taught Jane, and so on. A second series rectified this, and again included word identification, spelling pre-test, tutoring, and spelling post-test.

RESULTS For each of the three pupils, in each experimental sequence, one list had been learned as tutee, one list had been taught as tutor, and one list had not been met.

When the average scores of the three pupils were calculated from both sequences of the investigation, there was a gain of 59 per cent for words learned as tutee, and a gain of 47 per cent for words learned as tutor. Words not met as either tutee or tutor showed a 1 per cent loss.

DISCUSSION The investigators noted that tutoring another pupil can increase a pupil's spelling accuracy nearly as much as being tutored by another pupil. Additionally, the pupils themselves expressed a preference for tutoring as compared with independent study.

COMMENT In a sense, the two previous investigations were concerned with 'feeding back' information to pupils. This investigation differs, in that it was concerned with an instructional strategy, an area of research which has received a good deal of attention.

Learning to spell correctly is not the most exciting of tasks, and teachers have always sought ways to make the task more enjoyable. At the same time, there is an old saying which tends to reverberate around staffrooms that 'The way to learn a subject is to teach the subject'. The procedure used by Dineen, Clark and Risley used this approach. It proved to be successful with spelling. The extent to which this finding can be generalized to other pupils, and to other subjects, depends very much on the skill of future investigators.

Self-management

There has been a good deal of research on self-management in recent years, so much so, that O'Leary and O'Leary (1976) were able to subdivide the research into four main areas:

1 self-determination of goals and reinforcement standards;
2 self-recording;
3 self-evaluation;
4 self-reinforcement.

Self-determination of goals and standards

In self-determination, the pupils themselves are involved in selecting what is to be achieved (as was done at the Carr Hall centre), and when this has been done, the results obtained have been at least as successful as when goals are imposed upon the pupils. Nevertheless, as O'Leary and O'Leary (1976) emphasized, 'if relatively high standards are to be maintained, some surveillance and social reinforcement for high standard setting must be used'.

A good illustration of research involving self-determination of goals is seen in the work of Price and O'Leary (1974), when four five- to six-year-old pupils were treated for low academic performances. Initially, for five days, the pupils were given mathematics and reading problems consecutively, and asked to specify the number of problems they wished to complete. No reinforcement was given at this stage.

Following on from this, the pupils received social reinforcement (praise plus a hug or a pat on the back) for a 10 per cent increase in standard setting for mathematics alone. All four pupils increased the standard they set, and during a second baseline phase, in which no social reinforcement was given, the high standards were maintained, and generalized to the reading task.

Self-recording

Much of the work on self-recording has been very similar in kind to the investigations discussed earlier in this chapter (McNamara, 1979). However, the work of Dietz (1973) is worth emphasizing, since it was found that pupils aged eight to ten years deliberately mis-scored 15 per cent of their answers when self-recording. When a checking system was introduced, and then gradually faded out, less cheating was noted subsequently. This finding should serve to remind the reader of the earlier cautionary comments about potential cheating.

Self-evaluation

It may seem that self-recording and self-evaluation refer to the same process. However, the distinction between them is that whilst self-recording requires a pupil to count instances of a behaviour, self-evaluation requires the pupil to make a subjective estimate of his behaviour.

When research which uses self-evaluation by itself is examined, little effect is noted on disruptive behaviour, as O'Leary and O'Leary (1976) have noted. However, when self-evaluation has been built into a more extensive behaviour modification programme, involving other procedures, it has had promising results.

Drabman, Spitalnik and O'Leary (1973) worked with pupils who were regarded as 'emotionally disturbed'. The pupils were taught to evaluate their own behaviour on a rating scale.

Following a baseline phase in which the pupils' disruptive behaviour was observed, a treatment phase was introduced. During each day of the treatment phase, three 15-minute periods were designated as 'token periods', and one 15-minute period was designated as a 'control period'. During each token period, the pupils evaluated their own behaviour, awarding up to 5 points for appropriate social behaviour, such as keeping quiet, and up to 5 points for appropriate academic behaviour, such as completing work, and work correctly done. In the control periods, this procedure was not followed. Before each period commenced, the teacher told the pupils whether or not it was a token period.

Since one of the aims of the investigation was to encourage honest self-evaluation, the pupils' own self-evaluations were checked with the teachers' observations, and points were added or subtracted depending upon how closely the two sets of ratings matched.

The results showed a marked reduction in the pupils' disruptive behaviour both during the token periods and during the control periods.

Turkewitz, O'Leary and Ironsmith (1975) repeated the investigation with pupils aged seven to eleven, and obtained very similar results. However, they added a phase at the end of the investigation, in which the teacher's checking of ratings was faded out. The disruptive behaviour of the pupils remained low without being checked.

What seems to be particularly important in these two investigations, is the generalization which was demonstrated. The pupils behaved well during the lessons in which they did not receive tokens, that is, during the control lessons, and they behaved well after the teacher's checking was removed.

There is, however, another side to this story. In the investigation conducted by Turkewitz, O'Leary and Ironsmith, the pupils were treated in a special class, and although their disruptive behaviour decreased markedly in the special class, their disruptive behaviour did not decrease in their ordinary classrooms. To be fair, no attempt was made to encourage the pupils to use the techniques of self-evaluation in the ordinary classrooms, and had this been done, the results might have been very different.

Bearing this finding in mind, one cannot assume that self-evaluation will of itself produce generalization. However, it certainly does not seem to be a harmful procedure, and it may well be advantageous to build an element of self-evaluation into other treatment procedures, provided that it is externally monitored and that the skill is carefully developed.

Self-reinforcement

Self-reinforcement refers to self-selection of the consequences of behaviour; so that, for example, a person on a diet may decide to buy an outfit of clothes one size smaller than his present size, when a weight loss would make it feasible to wear the outfit.

There really appears to be no direct classroom research on the effects of self-reinforcement as defined here, although elements of the process are evident in many investigations, as in the case reported in this chapter (Presland, 1980), when the teacher of Virginia talked with the class and agreed that a letter would be sent to a pupil's parents, saying how well the pupil was doing. In a limited way, the pupils were using self-selection. However, there were very real limits on what they could select, and presumably this will always be so.

Despite a lack of direct research, there is no reason why pupils should not be taught to recognize small accomplishments, and to perhaps derive reinforcement from progress made. Indeed, it seems quite likely that many solitary workers do make progress in this way.

On a broader level, when reinforcers other than social reinforcers are to be employed, it does seem to be very useful to involve the pupils in the selection of the reinforcers. And whilst it is difficult to envisage that pupils would have an unlimited choice, it is very likely that, within the limitations that must apply in the classroom, the choices made by the pupils will act as more powerful reinforcers than would the choices made by the teacher.

General Discussion

From the selected examples which have been presented in this chapter, it should be apparent that behaviour modification techniques have been widely applied within schools. Moreover, it will have been seen that these techniques have been applied in a variety of ways by different investigators.

Each of the reports presented in the chapter has been summarised so that certain features might be emphasized. Naturally, some of these features required longer explanations than did others, so that the length and complexity of the reports varies considerably. For example, it was felt necessary to include details on the obtaining of percentage agreement when both a teacher and an independent observer recorded pupil behaviour, and when independent judges rated pupils' output. That such details are not included for all the investigations discussed, should not be taken to mean that they were not part of the original report, since, for example, when two observers record behaviour, the calculation of observer agreement is a routine procedure which is normally presented in the report of an investigation. Consequently, the space devoted here to each report has been dictated by considerations of the relevance of certain of its features to the concerns of this chapter.

The investigations in the primary and secondary schools which were discussed, do perhaps give the impression that similar procedures are both equally applicable and equally used in each kind of school. However, it must be remembered that investigations in the primary school which used social reinforcement were omitted from this chapter, and this is a very effective technique with many primary school pupils. That social reinforcement can be effective in the secondary school, is seen in the work of MacMillan and Kolvin (1977) which has been discussed, but such successful investigations are rarely reported, and indeed, in the same report, MacMillan and Kolvin themselves noted social reinforcement to be an ineffective treatment with another pupil.

When special schools were discussed, two establishments (Carr Hall, strictly speaking, was not a school) were described in which behaviour modification techniques were used very extensively, and whilst the discussion of the two establishments was intended to be informative, it should not be taken to imply that all special schools employ similar systems. In schools for ESN(M) pupils for example, the behaviour modification techniques which are used are often very similar to those which are employed in ordinary primary and secondary schools.

It may seem from the reports of modelling, academic performance, and self-management taken from other school systems, that the work being done outside this country is very different from that which concerns British investigators. This is not really the case. Much of the work done in other school systems is similar to the work undertaken in Britain, although there is so much behaviour modification research being conducted in schools elsewhere, particularly in the USA, that inevitably, a good deal of this work will differ from that in Britain. In this chapter, the aim has been to emphasize this difference in order to illustrate the diversity of the research; for fuller accounts of the work which has been undertaken on modelling, academic performance, and self-management, the reader might like to consult Yates and Yates (1978), Klein (1979), and Rosenbaum and Drabman (1979), respectively.

There are some quite marked differences to be seen in the specific aims of the various reported investigations. In many, a specific problem was tackled, for example, Ann's refusal to transfer to the infant school reception class (Yule, Berger and Wigley, 1977); whilst in others, a more general educational problem was examined, for example, the extent to which pupils' ability to write 'creative English' could be increased (Campbell and Willis, 1978). However, it would be unfortunate if the differences were allowed to obscure the similarities. In each of the investigations, the general aim was to improve the level of functioning of one or more pupils. Moreover, in each of the investigations, the behaviour of concern was defined, measured, and evaluated after treatment.

Whilst it is important to stress that behaviour modifiers have the same general aim, it is clear that they make use of different techniques and differing combinations of techniques. In part, these are determined by the kind of problem being investigated, and by the particular setting of the investigation. However, they are also determined by the various decisions which are made by the investigator, and it is quite likely that two different investigators would tackle the same problem in different ways, as was seen in the discussion of the work of Wheldall and Austin (1980), when one investigator favoured a 'rules, praise and ignoring' strategy, whilst the other favoured a 'game' strategy. Experimentation with different techniques is one of the means by which behaviour modification research progresses.

One interesting difference which is seen between behaviour modification research in Britain and in North America lies in the kind of reinforcement which is used. This may well be caused by cultural differences. It may not be apparent from the reports which have been discussed, but very often North American investigators make use of rather expensive back-up reinforcers, as was seen in the discussion of the work of Campbell and Willis (1978), in which pupils could trade in their tokens at a 'party'. The situation is very different in Britain. Here, the 'back-up' tends to be on a more modest scale – five minutes extra play-time, or a letter sent home – if indeed any back-up is used at all. And in view of the reported success of such investigations, it may well be that North American investigators have undervalued the power of lesser reinforcers. A system of expensive back-up reinforcers is not only wasteful but, more importantly, it may make the fading out of reinforcement difficult to achieve.

Whilst a number of the investigations which have been discussed have been concerned with the treatment of whole classes of pupils, care has been taken, whenever possible, to show individual pupil reactions, although these are not always reported by the investigators themselves when they seek to write concise, succinct reports. However, sufficient examples have been included to demonstrate that when the behaviour of a whole class is treated, it is unlikely that all the pupils will respond in the same way. In practice, of course, large gains can be made by treating whole classes, but whenever possible the needs of individual pupils must also be considered, and the best way of ensuring that this can be achieved is by including some form of individual measurement within an investigation.

One dimension along which the investigations seem to differ lies in the degree of pupil-involvement in the behaviour modification programmes. To be fair, however, when a research report does not mention pupil consultation, it cannot necessarily be concluded that pupil consultation did not take place, since there is a very real limit on how much detail an investigator can include in a research article. However, some of the published articles do explicitly detail such consultations, whilst others make no reference to discussions with pupils. Because of the many variables involved, for example, the kind of behaviour to be treated, and the school setting, it would be foolish to suggest that pupils should always be consulted about all aspects of a treatment programme. On the other hand, in view of the reported successes obtained when pupils were involved, for example, in recording their own behaviour, in agreeing contracts, and in selecting potential reinforcers, it would seem that pupil involvement can be very valuable in successful behaviour modification.

Finally, whilst many reports have been discussed which show the effective use of behaviour modification in schools, no attempt has been made to hide the difficulties which have been encountered. In one (Wheldall and Austin, 1980), the investigators had difficulty in persuading teachers to work with them, and in another (Merrett and Wheldall, 1978), the teacher said she 'felt silly' putting up a chart of rules. One investigation produced results which are at best 'encouraging' (Harrop, 1977a), and in another, the results did not generalize from a special class into the pupils' ordinary classroom (Turkewitz, O'Leary and Ironsmith, 1975). In yet another report (McNamara, 1979), of the three pupils who were treated by self-recording, only two showed marked improvements. These difficulties are stressed because much can be learned from them. A balanced appraisal needs to include an element of 'what went wrong?', as well as 'what went right?'

In summary, it should be evident that classroom behaviour modifiers, when they are confronted with problems, now have a considerable background of research upon which they can draw. Since pupils and situations differ, as do the investigators themselves, there is no prescribed way for tackling each problem; yet, whilst different investigations may involve differing practices, the underlying principles will remain the same.

Chapter 7

Critical Comments, Questions and Answers

Talking with teachers about behaviour modification in the early 1970s was an exciting activity. Reactions varied from, 'This is monstrous, I've never heard anything like it before', to, 'But surely this is what teachers always do.' Such was the variety of response that I was forced to the conclusion that individual differences between teachers were at least as great as the individual differences between their pupils.

In more recent years, there has been a diminution in the cries of outrage, and a more considered, less emotional response has been observable. This is probably due to a greater awareness among teachers of the real meaning of behaviour modification, arising from the increased availability of literature and the growth of in-service courses. Some teachers, it is true, will become acquainted with the approach during initial training, but even in recent times, this acquaintance is unlikely to have extended beyond listening to a couple of lectures, as a survey conducted by Schwieso and Hastings (1981) indicates.

Over the years, I have been asked many questions about behaviour modification, and have given many answers. In an effort to deal with some of the doubts and uncertainties which may still linger in the reader's mind, this chapter provides a consideration of some of the issues most frequently raised in my experience.

Some of these perennial questions of course, have already been dealt with in previous chapters, and there would seem to be little point in repeating, for example, my discussion of whether it is possible to 'really' change a pupil's behaviour when his home environment merely serves to reinforce his inappropriate conduct.

Those questions to which I address myself in this final chapter seem to me of equal importance, and obviously reflect genuine worries and uncertainties on the part of those interested in the practice of behaviour modification. It is natural and healthy that good teachers should be sincerely concerned about their interactions with pupils, and with the processes involved in these interactions. The questions and answers which follow represent an attempt to remove some of the most frequently-met uncertainties and anxieties. It should be remembered, however, that the answers are merely expressions of one writer's opinions.

Behaviour Modification seems to be Based upon Bribing Pupils

This is perhaps the most frequently voiced of all the criticisms – implied or explicit – of behaviour modification. As such it cannot go unanswered, although in a limited sense an answer was given in Chapter 1, during my consideration of the treatment of Teddy, who was allowed to earn model cars by increasing his work output. At that point I was chiefly concerned with demonstrating the discrepancy between the commonly accepted definition of bribery and the procedures used in behaviour modification. However, even when they acknowledge this discrepancy, teachers still tend to feel uneasy about the use of such rewards. A personal anecdote may help to pinpoint some of the reasons for unease.

As a probationary teacher in a secondary modern school many years ago, I was taken to task by a senior teacher for awarding house points to some of the pupils in the final year, lowest stream class, for sitting at their desks and working quietly during the lesson. This, the senior teacher patiently explained, was precisely what the pupils were supposed to be doing, and as such, it was not a behaviour worthy of specific reward. House points were given for behaviour above and beyond this normal level. He was completely unimpressed by the counter-argument that sitting, working quietly, was not the usual behaviour of all these pupils during my lesson.

Who was right? Reluctantly, I have to admit that the senior teacher was right. A probationary teacher was acting in a manner contrary to the school's customary practices, and such behaviour could have had an adverse effect on the usefulness of the existing house-point system. On the other hand, I don't believe myself to have been completely at fault in attempting to reward the pupils for appropriate working behaviour – and it should be added that this was a decade before I read about behaviour modification.

The view expressed by the senior teacher, that pupils should not be rewarded for behaving as they are supposed to behave, is held by many members of the teaching profession.

On the other hand, teachers themselves expect to be rewarded for behaving as they are supposed to behave, and they are not content to be rewarded at a mere subsistence level. Like members of any other professional group, they submit their pay claims in due season, and their whole promotional ladder is tied to increases in salary. It almost seems as if there is an element of 'double-standards' here. The teacher expects to be rewarded for appropriate behaviour, but does not feel that the pupil should be treated in the same way.

It could be argued that the teacher needs a salary to exist, and that the pupil's existence is ensured by his parents. However, teachers are not normally content with a salary which merely allows them to exist; they wish to live in a manner which is commensurate with the work they do.

If we take this discussion a stage further, teachers often feel that the work they do in the classroom is of little consequence in determining promotion, and that what is done and said outside the classroom has a disproportionate influence on their future prospects. This feeling indicates that teachers would like to be rewarded for what they know to be their most important function – teaching their pupils. Is it, then, so unreasonable that pupils should be rewarded for their most important function – learning from their teachers?

In many ways, the rewards obtained by teachers and pupils are similar in kind. Teachers tend to appreciate and respond to approving comments from their head-teachers about work well done; and, in exactly the same way, many pupils will respond to positive comments and compliments from their teacher. However, for some pupils, for a variety of reasons, positive comments from the teacher do not seem to be rewarding, and for such pupils the teacher who uses the principles of behaviour modification initially endeavours to find rewards which are available within the normal teaching environment. If he is unable to find such rewards, however, he may have to employ more 'artificial' rewards. When this is done, the treatment has at least two main aims: one is to improve the pupils' behaviour, and the other is to enable the pupils to find the teacher's attention to be rewarding.

This analysis of rewards does of necessity over-simplify the aims of behaviour modification treatment, since as has been previously stressed, one must not neglect the academic 'diet' of the pupils. If we assume that a teacher has done all that he can to ensure that a pupil is receiving an appropriate curriculum, then a pupil who behaves inappropriately in the classroom will need, at least in the short-term, to be rewarded by measures external to the curriculum itself.

That pupils should occupy themselves with tasks which are educationally beneficial, because they find the tasks to be rewarding, is what one would hope to find in the classroom. However, many tasks require that a pupil develops certain skills before such rewards can be derived. Some tasks, like drawing and painting, may be rewarding even in the earlier stages of a developing skill, but in other tasks, the earlier stages may be so different from the final product that they seem to embody little 'natural' reward. Reading is probably the best example of a skill which has little rewarding value in its early stages, whilst in the latter stages, considerable reward can be gained from the appreciation of a story.

It is when the pupil is learning basic skills that he is most likely to need rewards which are external to the task itself. If he is not so rewarded, then even the most eager pupil is unlikely to make fully satisfactory progress.

It may be that, despite this extended discussion, there are still some teachers who object to rewarding pupils for appropriate classroom behaviour. Given that it is their function to teach pupils, it would be interesting to know what alternatives they would offer. When teachers have pupils in their classrooms whose behaviour leaves room for improvement, the teachers have a duty to help such pupils. If they reject behaviour modification because they feel uneasy about feelings of bribery, the onus is on them to offer an alternative, successful, workable treatment.

Why should We reward Pupils who are Nuisances in Class?

This question, frequently asked, often implies the accusation of bribery which has just been discussed. Sometimes, however, it also embodies the concept of blame, that is, the feeling that failure to work, or active misbehaviour in class is the pupil's own fault.

It is perhaps not difficult to see how a teacher's exasperation at a pupil's behaviour can lead him to this view but, quite frankly, I believe that such reasoning can be both dangerous and irresponsible. It can be dangerous because it tends to divert the teacher from trying to help the pupil, and it can be irresponsible because it may lead him to neglect the full performance of his teaching function.

Provided the pupil ought to be in the classroom, it is the teacher's duty to teach him, and to help alleviate his difficulties. Blame is an irrelevant consideration, and can even be a convenient way for a teacher to rationalize a serious problem out of existence.

What gives the Teacher the Right to Modify a Pupil's Behaviour?

To answer this question we need to examine what a teacher does in the classroom. He is there to teach. Teaching involves following a curriculum, selecting appropriate materials, explaining, discussing, setting work, marking work, and a host of allied functions. The teacher performs these activities in order to promote the well-being of his pupils in the widest possible sense. This is his duty.

When the teacher performs these duties, he is modifying the behaviour of his pupils. Their behaviours will change as a consequence of his behaviour. They will learn in accordance with the quality of his teaching. If he selects material appropriate to their level of understanding, if he is seen to be a 'rewarding' person, and gives his approval for work well done, they will learn. In short, whether he is aware of it or not, he is using the practices of behaviour modification.

When the teacher systematically applies the principles of behaviour modification, he is fulfilling his duty. He has an obligation to promote the well-being of the pupils in his class, and he is responding to that obligation.

Despite a general agreement with such arguments, it is sometimes evident that individual teachers nevertheless feel uneasy about putting the principles of behaviour modification into practice in a systematic manner. There is a strange, almost perverse, reluctance to employ procedures which are efficient and workable.

This is a difficult feeling to counter, and it may be that these teachers feel a moral objection to such deliberate attempts to change a pupil's behaviour. This is a perfectly understandable attitude, and yet it should be borne in mind that talking with a difficult pupil, guiding him, advising him, and reasoning with him, are all strategies aimed at achieving the same end. Regardless of the way these processes are described, they are all used in an attempt to influence the pupil, and to bring about a change in behaviour.

Behaviour Modification denies Freedom of Choice

If this statement implies that individuals normally make absolutely free choices without being influenced by their genetic make-up and by their personal histories, then the statement is accurate.

Behaviour modifiers take a different view of human behaviour, however. Behaviour modification is primarily concerned with the ways in which experiences, individual responses, and the consequences of these responses influence behaviour. In short, the behaviour modifier sees man as being a creature responsive to his environment, rather than independent of it.

This viewpoint clearly recognizes the uniqueness of each individual, since each human being has a genetic endowment and an environmental history which is uniquely his own; and it may be recalled that behaviour modification investigations lay considerable stress on individual reactions to treatment.

At a superficial level, some behaviour modification programmes have certainly restricted individual freedom. In the investigations which have been described in the earlier chapters, pupils have learned not to interrupt their teachers, and not to interrupt other pupils when they are working. On the other hand, these same pupils have learned to respect the rights of others, to learn from the teacher, and from the material he presents. Other pupils have learned not to sit passively in class, and to ask questions when they require help. With the increased learning which can ensue comes increased choice, in both the educational and the vocational senses.

Granting freedom of choice to pupils surely does not extend to giving them freedom to do as they will, without regard to long-term consequences. Unfortunately, much heedless, short-sighted behaviours can result from the random effects of short-term rewards. To take an extreme yet pertinent example, the end-product of short-term 'freedoms' may well turn out to be innumeracy and illiteracy – a sad outcome for the pupil, leaving him severely incapacitated in modern society, with very real restrictions on his ultimate, long-term freedom of choice. It therefore becomes the teacher's inescapable responsibility to select short-term rewards designed to facilitate the sort of pupil behaviours which will eventuate in the long-term rewards of increased educational and vocational 'freedom'.

Many behaviour modification programmes stress the importance of drawing the pupils' attention to the rules of the classroom. For this to be fully effective, the rules need to be thoroughly explained, clarified and kept constantly in mind by the pupils. With many classes, however, these procedures might well be taken a stage further: the rules could be jointly formulated by teacher and pupils. Such 'participation', in giving the pupils a certain freedom of choice, would surely enhance their sense of responsibility for their own behaviour, and enable them to witness and experience at close hand, in however limited a sense, the practical workings of democracy.

In general terms, it seems important that care should be taken not to equate freedom for the pupil with an abdication from planning and foresight on the part of the teacher. Leaving the pupil at the mercy of random rewards and ill-considered immediate 'freedoms' may all too easily result in ultimate restrictions to more desirable long-term freedoms.

Isn't there a Danger that Behaviour Modification Techniques can be Abused?

It has already been mentioned that using behaviour modification to 'prop up' a poor curriculum would be an abuse of its techniques. Behaviour modification is admittedly no more immune to abuse than such human advances as television, healing drugs, and similar scientific discoveries.

The key to avoiding abuse would seem to be openness. Procedures need to be discussed, publicized and scrutinized.

Another potential form of abuse lies in the use of behaviour modification techniques by those who do not fully understand the principles and the procedures. This is one of the reasons why numerous in-service courses in behaviour modification have been conducted, such as those quoted by Merritt (1981), and run by Harrop, Critchley and McNamara in Liverpool, Yule, Berger and Wigley in Inner London, Firman and Hastings in Berkshire, Cook in Glasgow, and Merrett in the West Midlands.

In spite of the dangers of abuse – indeed, precisely because of these dangers – it seems important to encourage the spread of knowledge of behaviour modification principles and procedures as widely as possible among the teaching profession. It is surely desirable that such a useful method of influencing pupils' behaviour should be practised by as many teachers as can be trained to become expert in its use. In my view, more harm to pupils may arise from a teacher's non-use or misuse of behaviour modification than from its expert application in appropriate circumstances.

Does Good Teaching necessarily involve the Practice of Behaviour Modification?

It is often asserted that 'good teachers are born, not made'. If this were true, a good deal of teacher-education would seem to be irrelevant and therefore dispensable. Careful observation of student teachers during the course of various teaching practices, however, appears to disprove this assertion. Nevertheless, it must be conceded that marked individual differences continue to exist between different student teachers.

Many individuals come to teaching with certain in-built advantages. Considered at the descriptive level, they frequently appear to appreciate the needs of their pupils, liking and respecting them, and being liked and respected in their turn. Often they appear to enjoy the actual teaching process. When these characteristics are combined with such features as an enthusiasm for learning and an extensive knowledge of available and appropriate curriculum material, they appear to complete the picture of a good teacher.

Implicit in this picture are some of the typical features of the potentially successful behaviour modifier. Ideally, the latter will select a curriculum appropriate to his pupils' level of performance, and present it in such a way as to be 'reinforcing' to them. If the material presented does not reinforce the pupils, there will be no need to search for 'external reinforcers' so long as the teacher's attention itself will act as a reinforcer.

If the pupils' resultant appropriate behaviour in its turn serves to reinforce the teacher (and it should always be remembered that behaviour modification is a reciprocal process), then the teacher will be more likely to have enthusiastic, respectful pupils in his class, than is a teacher who shows neither enthusiasm for learning nor respect for his pupils.

The teacher who comes to his task with the sort of in-built qualities I have described, obviously starts at an advantage, both as a teacher and a potential behaviour modifier. The important thing, however, is not so much his advantages or his potentialities, as his ability to learn from the classroom situation itself. All too often one sees a potentially good teacher squandering his in-built advantages by failing to acquire anything more than a cursory knowledge of appropriate curriculum material, and by neglecting to set adequate learning goals for his pupils.

Pupils taught by a good teacher are given an appropriate curriculum. They know which rules are to be observed. They are selectively reinforced for appropriate behaviour, and they have in their teacher an appropriate model to imitate. Such a teacher is using the principles of behaviour modification.

Very many teachers already teach in this way, without having any explicit knowledge of behaviour modification principles, and indeed, this is only to be expected since teachers, as we have seen, are reinforced by the appropriate behaviour of their pupils. However, one of the ever-present threats to continued good teaching is complacency, and improvement is always possible. Perhaps a personal anecdote will make this clearer.

Before setting up the investigation with Mr Brown, the teacher of Tom, whose case is described in Chapter 1, I first sought the permission of his head teacher. He readily gave this, but warned me that the investigation would be a waste of time, since Mr Brown was a first-class teacher, who was already 'working wonders' with his pupils. The head was right in the sense that Mr Brown was, and still is, a first class teacher, but wrong in the sense that Mr Brown's subsequent treatment of Tom turned out to be extremely successful. In this particular case, Mr Brown's use of social reinforcement had been inadequate in dealing with Tom's difficulties. He needed to make use of a more specific procedure, that of making a contract, before he was able to effect an improvement in Tom's behaviour.

To summarize, I would suggest not only that the good teacher constantly makes use of behaviour modification principles and practices, whether consciously or otherwise, but also that he can become an even better teacher as he grows more fully acquainted with the procedures which may be employed.

What Happens to the Pupil who Moves to another Teacher after his Behaviour has been Successfully Modified?

The result of successful behaviour modification is that the pupil who previously had difficulties in the classroom comes to behave in the same way as his classroom peers, given the same conditions of reinforcement. When this final stage is reached, the pupil may well be at no greater risk than his peers of reverting to earlier inappropriate behaviour. Nevertheless, it must be remembered that such a pupil has only recently learned to behave appropriately under normal conditions of reinforcement, and that therefore his learning is likely to be more easily disrupted by a changing pattern of teaching than is the learning of his peers.

Sometimes it may not be possible to reach this final stage in behaviour modification before the pupil moves to another teacher. When this occurs, the disruption caused by such a movement can be considerable. This is a situation which needs to be avoided if possible, but it may well occur when a pupil's difficulties are slow to respond to treatment, or to the fading out of treatment.

The best way to minimize any disruption caused by a pupil moving from one teacher to another is to ensure accurate communication of what procedures have been used with the pupil, and what has been achieved. Under ideal circumstances, one teacher might well continue where the other left off. To an extent, this can often be achieved when a pupil moves within a school, but it is more difficult when a pupil is transferred from one school to another.

In practical terms, it is not easy to conduct long-term evaluations of pupils' progress in subsequent classes. Even if the range of pupil behaviours of concern were the same as those formerly observed, one could not expect to impose the original observers on a new teacher, at specific times in the day. However, behaviour modifiers do check informally on the further progress of pupils whose behaviour has been modified, and by and large such progress has tended to be very satisfactory. Without the information gleaned from such checks, few would continue to practise behaviour modification.

Whilst it has to be admitted that difficulties may arise when a pupil whose behaviour has been successfully modified moves from one teacher to another, this does not weaken the gains that behaviour modification can produce in the classroom. As in all walks of life, the pupil must move from one sphere of influence to another, and the teacher's task is to prepare the pupil as best he can for his move to another teacher. The teacher's ultimate aim for a pupil who has experienced difficulties in the classroom is the alleviation of such difficulties, so that the pupil no longer requires special treatment.

If this is accompanied by accurate communication with the pupil's subsequent teacher, and by later, informal contacts, the pupil is being given increased opportunities for successful adjustment.

Behaviour Modification is too Simple

When this criticism refers to the practices and procedures of behaviour modification, it is usually made by individuals who have little knowledge of what is involved. In view of what has been written in earlier chapters, it would seem unnecessary to attempt to answer such objections with an extended discussion. Whether or not the accusation is just must be decided by the reader for himself, from the evidence already presented.

Sometimes, however, this criticism reflects a rather different view of psychology – usually that of psychoanalysis, which sees inappropriate behaviour as a symptom of an underlying disease. Such a view suggests that the mere changing of overt behaviour has little or no effect on the disease; if the inappropriate behaviour is removed, another will take its place. In other words, one symptom is substituted for another.

Like much of psychoanalysis, this kind of reasoning seems superficially persuasive. However, as Brown (1978) has noted, 'The facts are that unambiguous evidence of symptom-substitution has yet to be found during behaviour modification intervention.'

Whilst the idea of symptom-substitution as a manifestation of an underlying disease is rejected by behaviour modifiers, it is recognized that the employment of behaviour modification techniques may result in unusual pupil behaviours. This can result in the phenomenon of the 'storm before the calm', discussed in Chapter 1. When the reinforcement which a pupil has obtained for inappropriate behaviour is removed from that particular behaviour, it is quite likely that he will respond initially in a variety of ways, in an effort to extract reinforcement. This is not symptom-substitution, but simply the normal course of learning.

It may be easy to criticize behaviour modification, but if criticism is to move beyond the level of mere theorizing, it must produce evidence which can be observed. If we turn the original statement around, criticism and speculation are simple; producing evidence is more complex.

Behaviour Modification is too Complex

The short answer to this observation is that behaviour modification can in practice be relatively simple to undertake, or it can involve a complex design which includes a number of procedures. The degree of complexity depends upon such features as the aim of the investigation, who is undertaking it, and the resources available for recording. This should become readily apparent when the various cases reported are compared with one another.

Those who voice this criticism sometimes imply that the procedures in which the teacher engages, particularly the recording of a pupil's behaviour, take time away from teaching pupils. On the face of it, this seems a reasonable objection; recording does take time. In answer to this, Brown (1978) has made three cogent points. He emphasizes the need for evaluation; he points out that the time spent in observing and recording need not be lengthy; and he stresses that taking the trouble to observe the behaviour of a pupil systematically enables the teacher to get to know him very well.

In short, the time taken in systematic observation is time well spent, and the benefits obtained would seem to outweigh any inconvenience experienced.

How can Teachers initiate Behaviour Modification in Schools?

There are a number of ways in which this can be accomplished. At perhaps the simplest level, reading about behaviour modification will tend to alert the teacher to such considerations as classroom rules, and the effects of reinforcement on his relationship and interaction with pupils.

At a more complex level, teachers may wish to undertake systematic programmes with individual pupils. There is, at this point, always a danger of too simple an approach being taken. It could be, for example, that the pupil's curriculum is ignored, or that no thought is given to the fading out of an artificial system of reinforcement. The possibility of such naïve applications prompted Berger (1979) to warn of the dangers of a mindless technology, leading to potential misuse of behaviour modification. Such warnings should not discourage the potential practitioner, but they do serve to underline the importance of a careful appraisal of the principles and practices involved, of attending in-service courses, and of consulting where possible, with educational psychologists. One would hope that the teacher with a genuine concern for the difficulties of any of his pupils would express this concern by finding out as much as he could about behaviour modification before deciding to use its techniques.

If we return to the original question posed, the first step is to obtain as much information about behaviour modification as possible, by whatever means are available, and then to plan a programme. Whenever other members of a school's staff are involved, consultation is necessary, and the degree of consultation depends upon the degree of involvement. Should a whole school staff be concerned, a staff-meeting would seem to be the appropriate occasion for discussion. The educational psychologist ought to be involved at this stage, and from him, or through him, expert advice can be obtained.

How Useful is it to have Observers other than the Teacher in the Classroom?

Observers can be useful in a variety of ways, some of which have already been discussed. At the beginning of an investigation an observer can be employed to see if defined categories of behaviour can be accurately observed, and the percentage agreement between the teacher and the observer can be calculated, to yield a measure of accuracy. This procedure can, of course, be continued throughout an investigation. Having no other demands on his attention, however, the observer is perhaps best utilized for more extensive recording of behaviour than the teacher could accomplish unaided.

By the same token, two observers in support of the teacher are frequently better than one. This is because each observer can be used as a 'check' on the other. In the interests of experimental rigour, the two observers ought to make their observations independently, keeping their recordings separate throughout an investigation – though the investigator himself, of course, should maintain a constant check upon their findings.

Further precautions may be necessary to guard against the possibility of observers inadvertently 'seeing' simply what they expect to see. One such measure might be to keep them in ignorance of the full and precise details of the experimental procedures; and – as a further step – it might be prudent to suggest to the observers, from the outset, that a prime objective of the investigation is to examine levels of agreement obtained from independent observations. When this was done in a recent investigation (Harrop, 1979), no evidence was found that observers produced recordings in line with prior expectations.

In spite of the undoubted advantages accruing from the use of observers, however, there is one undeniable problem which it poses. Their presence in a classroom does alter the environment, even though the effects of this can be minimized to a certain extent if the pupils have had the opportunity to become accustomed to such 'outsiders' as student teachers, classroom assistants, helpers and the like. Nevertheless, some departure from the norms of classroom behaviour is inevitable in the presence of special observers, and it is advisable for the teacher to attempt to 'measure' this, as far as possible, by systematic checks undertaken both before their arrival and throughout their stay in the classroom.

In normal circumstances, of course, teachers are not likely to be able to obtain the services of observers, but this should not cause undue concern. Teachers can make observations during the normal process of teaching and, with a little careful planning, they can record a good deal of information about their pupils with comparative ease. True, there will be no independent checks on their recordings, but when the aim of an investigation is to alleviate the difficulties experienced by one or more pupils in the classroom, who can evaluate the results better than the teacher?

Conclusions

I am conscious of having raised a host of questions about behaviour modification in the classroom, and hope likewise to have offered acceptable answers to a few of them. Nevertheless, other questions will no doubt remain in the reader's mind, some of them possibly triggered off by the very answers I have put forward. This is as it should be. It may be that some of the questions have been prompted by imperfections in my argument or in my proferred answers. If so, apologies are due. Questioning is the surest way of progress, however, and more satisfactory answers should be sought by further reading, and by appropriate questioning of established practitioners of behaviour modification.

Where does Behaviour Modification go from Here?

Any answer to this question must necessarily be speculative, and one can only look for 'clues' in the experience of the past and the present.

If we examine the development of behaviour modification in schools, we observe a progressive increase in the number of investigations reported. Concomitant with this, we see its techniques being applied to a wider variety of pupil behaviours, and there are signs that the pupils themselves are being increasingly involved in the decision-making processes inherent in the modification procedures. Teachers are acquiring ever greater knowledge and expertise, mainly through the emergence of in-service courses.

Similar expansion may be expected until behaviour modification becomes school-based. The seeds of this development are already evident in the work of Yule, Berger and Wigley (1977), who have been working on a 'Teacher-Child Interaction Project' in order to enable teachers to pass on behavioural skills to other teachers.

If we examine the present, and look at education in general, it is apparent that we are in a period of uncertainty and transition. Schools are being closed, amalgamated and reorganized, and a feeling of impermanence is being engendered by the clash of opposing political philosophies. The curriculum is being examined for relevance, and there is evidence of a swing back to previously discarded beliefs. Adolescence, always a period of restless inquiry, seems to be the focus of almost unprecedented conflict today. The lack of stability in our society is clearly being reflected in our schools.

Alongside this uncertainty and change, there is an increased questioning of the procedures and practices within our schools. Much of this has been concerned with the use of punishment. Whilst this is vigorously attacked on humanitarian grounds, there is also strong evidence in the work of Rutter *et al.* (1979), which has been referred to a number of times in Chapter 3, suggesting that it is reward rather than punishment which is effective in producing improved behaviour in schools. If we add to this the successes reported by behaviour modifiers, as typified in the various investigations cited in this book, it may become apparent that a diminution in the intensity and frequency of punishment could well be accompanied by an increased, informed use of the principles of behaviour modification, to the mutual benefit of pupils, teachers, and society at large.

References

BARRISH, H. H., SAUNDERS, M. and WOLF, M. M. (1969) 'Good behavior game: effects of individual contingencies for group consequences on disruptive behavior in the classroom'. *Journal of Applied Behavior Analysis*, 2, 119–24.

BERGER, M. (1979) 'Behaviour modification in education and professional practice: the dangers of a mindless technology'. *Bulletin of the British Psychological Society*, 32, 418–19.

BROWN, B. J. (1978) 'How to win the "putdown-B-M" game and influence people'. *Newsletter of the Association for Behaviour Modification with Children*, 2, 8–10.

BURLAND, J. R. (1979) 'Behaviour modification in a residential school for junior maladjusted boys: an overview'. *Journal of the Association of Workers with Maladjusted Children*, 7, 65–79.

BURNS, R. B. (1978) 'The relative effectiveness of various incentives and deterrents as judged by pupils and teachers'. *Educational Studies*, 4, 3, 229–43.

CAMPBELL, J. A. and WILLIS, J. (1978) 'Modifying components of "creative behaviour" in the natural environment'. *Behavior Modification*, 2, 549–64.

CHAPMAN, T. (1981) *Self concept and pupil performance. A theoretical and empirical analysis*. Unpublished Ph.D. thesis, University of Lancaster.

CLARIZIO, H. F. and YELON, S. L. (1967) 'Learning theory approaches to classroom management: rationale and intervention'. *Journal of Special Education*, 1, 267–74.

DIETZ, A. (1973) *The effects of teacher feedback on veridicality of self-evaluation on an individualized reading task*. Unpublished undergraduate honors study, SUNY, Stony Brook, New York.

DINEEN, J. P., CLARK, H. B. and RISLEY, T. R. (1977) 'Peer tutoring among elementary students: educational benefits to the tutor'. *Journal of Applied Behavior Analysis*, 10, 231–8.

DRABMAN, R. S., SPITALNIK, R. and O'LEARY, K. D. (1973) 'Teaching self-control to disruptive children'. *Journal of Abnormal Psychology* 82, 10–16.

ENTWISTLE, N. J. (1972) 'Personality and academic attainment'. *British Journal of Educational Psychology*, 42, 137–51.

FRIEDRICH, L. K. and STEIN, A. H. (1973) 'Aggressive and prosocial television programes and the natural behavior of preschool children'. *Monographs of the Society for Research in Child Development*, 38, No. 4.

HARROP, L. A. (1977a) *The methodology and applications of contingency management in schools*. Unpublished Ph.D. thesis, University of Liverpool.

HARROP, L. A. (1977b) 'The vanishing problem'. *Quarterly Bulletin of the British Association for Behavioural Psychotherapy*, 5, 3, 51–5.

HARROP, L. A. (1978a) 'Another gain for the modifiers?' *Special Education: Forward Trends*, 5, 4, 15–17.

HARROP, L. A. (1978b) 'Behaviour modification in the ordinary school setting'. *Association of Educational Psychologists Journal*, 4, 7, 3–15.

HARROP, L. A. (1979) 'An examination of observer bias in a classroom behaviour modification experiment'. *Educational Studies*, 5, 2, 97–107.

HARROP, L. A. and CRITCHLEY, C. (1972) 'Classroom management and deviant behaviour'. *Behaviour Modification*, 3, 6–10.

HARROP, L. A. and MCNAMARA, E. (1979) 'The behavioural workshop for classroom problems: a re-appraisal'. *British Journal of In-Service Education*, 5, 32–8.

HOMME, L. (1969) *How to Use Contingency Contracting in the Classroom*. Champaign, Ill.: Research Press.

KLEIN, R. D. (1979) 'Modifying academic performance in the grade school classroom; in HERSEN, M., EISLER, R. M. and MILLER, P. M. (eds) *Progress in Behavior Modification*, 8. New York: Academic Press.

LIVESLEY, W. J. and BROMLEY, D. (1973) *Person Perception in Childhood and Adolescence*. London: John Wiley and Sons.

LOVAAS, O. I., BERBERICH, J. P., PERLOFF, B. F. and SCHAEFFER, B. (1966) 'Acquisition of imitative speech in schizophrenic children'. *Science*, 151, 705–7

MacMILLAN, A. and KOLVIN, I. (1977) 'Behaviour modification in educational settings: a guide for teachers'. *Journal of the Association of Workers with Maladjusted Children*, 5, 2–18.

MCNAMARA, E. (1977) 'Results and impressions of using behaviour modification in a schools' psychological service – a personal view'. *Quarterly Bulletin of the British Association for Behavioural Psychotherapy*, 5, 3, 55–62.

MCNAMARA, E. (1978) *Management of problem behaviour through self-recording techniques*. Unpublished M.Sc. thesis, University of Manchester.

MCNAMARA, E. (1979) 'The use of self-recording in behaviour modification in a secondary school'. *Behavioural Psychotherapy*, 7, 57–66.

MCNAMARA, E. and MOORE, B. (1978) 'Special education treatment for maladjusted pupils in a day centre'. *Association of Educational Psychologists Journal*, 4, 15–20.

MADSEN, C. H., BECKER, W. C. and THOMAS, D. R. (1968) 'Rules, praise, and ignoring: elements of elementary classroom control'. *Journal of Applied Behavior Analysis*, 1, 139–50.

MERRETT, F. E. (1981) 'Studies in behaviour modification in British educational settings'. *Educational Psychology*, **1**, 1, 13–38.

MERRETT, F. E. and WHELDALL, K. (1978) 'Playing the game: a behavioural approach to classroom management in the junior school'. *Educational Review*, **30**, 1, 41–50.

O'CONNOR, R. D. (1969) 'Modification of social withdrawal through symbolic modeling'. *Journal of Applied Behavior Analysis*, 2, 15–22.

O'LEARY, S. G. and O'LEARY, K. D. (1976) Behavior modification in the school, in LEITENBERG, H. (ed.) *Handbook of Behavior Modification and Behavior Therapy*, New Jersey: Prentice-Hall.

POWELL, J., MARTINDALE, B., KULP, S., MARTINDALE, A. and BAUMAN, R. (1977) 'Taking a closer look: time sampling and measurement error'. *Journal of Applied Behavior Analysis*, 10, 325–32.

PRESLAND, J. L. (1980) 'Behaviour modification and secondary schools', in UPTON, G. and GOBELL, A. (eds) *Behaviour Problems in the Comprehensive School*. Faculty of Education, University College Cardiff.

PRICE, G. and O'LEARY, K. D. (1974) *Teaching children to develop high performance standards*. Unpublished manuscript, SUNY, Stony Brook, New York.

ROSENBAUM, M. S. and DRABMAN, R. S. (1979) 'Self-control training in the classroom: a review and critique'. *Journal of Applied Behavior Analysis*, 12, 467–85.

RUTTER, M., MAUGHAN, B., MORTIMORE, P. and OUSTON, J. (1979) *Fifteen Thousand Hours*. Shepton Mallet: Open Books.

SCHWIESO, J. and HASTINGS, N. (1981) 'The role of theory in the teaching of behaviour modification to teachers', in WHELDALL, K. (ed.) *The Behaviourist in the Classroom* Educational Review Offset Publications No. 1. Birmingham.

SKINNER, B. F. (1968) *The Technology of Teaching*. New York: Appleton-Century-Crofts.

THOMAS, J. D., PRESLAND, I. E., GRANT, M. D. and GLYNN, T. L. (1978) 'Natural rates of teacher approval and disapproval in grade-7 classrooms'. *Journal of Applied Behavior Analysis*, 11, 91–4.

TORRANCE, E. P. (1962) *Guiding Creative Talent.* New Jersey: Prentice-Hall.

TORRANCE, E. P. (1966) *Torrance Tests of Creative Thinking: Direction Manual and Scoring Guide*, New Jersey: Personnel Press.

TSOI M. M. and YULE, W. (1976) 'The effects of group reinforcement in classroom behaviour modification'. *Educational Studies*, **2**, 2, 129–40.

TURKEWITZ, H., O'LEARY, K. D. and IRONSMITH, M. (1975) 'Generalization and maintenance of appropriate behavior through self-control'. *Journal of Consulting and Clinical Psychology*, 43, 577–83.

VAN HOUTEN, R. V. and MCKILLOP, C. (1977) 'An extension of the effects of the performance feedback system with secondary school students'. *Psychology in the Schools*, **14**, 480–4.

WARD, J. (1971) 'Modification of children's deviant classroom behaviour'. *British Journal of Educational Psychology*, 41, 304–13.

WARD, J. (1973) 'The use of teacher attention and praise as control techniques in the classroom'. *Educational Review*, 26, 39–55.

WEST, M. M. and AXELROD, S. (1975) 'A 3D program for LD children'. *Academic Therapy*, 10, 309–19.

WHELDALL, K. and AUSTIN, R. (1980) 'Successful behaviour modification in the secondary school: a reply to McNamara and Harrop'. *British Psychological Society Division of Educational and Child Psychology Occasional Papers*, 4, 3–9.

WHELDALL, K., MORRIS, M., VAUGHAN, P. and NG, Y. Y. (1981) 'Rows versus tables: an example of the use of behavioural ecology in two classes of eleven-year-old children'. *Educational Psychology*, **1**, 2, 171–84.

WHITE, M. A. (1975) 'Natural rates of teacher approval and disapproval in the classroom'. *Journal of Applied Behavior Analysis*, 8, 367–72.

YATES, G. C. R. and YATES, S. M. (1978) 'The implications of social modelling research for education'. *The Australian Journal of Education*, **22**, 2, 161–78.

YULE, W., BERGER, M. and WIGLEY, V. (1977) 'The teacher-child interaction project'. *Quarterly Bulletin of the British Association for Behavioural Psychotherapy*, **5**, 3, 42–7.

Index